YOU WILL BE ABLE TO DRAW BY THE END OF THIS BOOK.

An Hachette UK Company
www.hachette.co.uk

First published in Great Britain in 2017 by
Ilex, an imprint of
Octopus Publishing Group Ltd
Carmelite House
50 Victoria Embankment
London EC4Y 0DZ
www.octopusbooks.co.uk

Distributed in the US by
Hachette Book Group
1290 Avenue of the Americas
4th and 5th Floors
New York, NY 10020

Distributed in Canada by
Canadian Manda Group
664 Annette St.
Toronto, Ontario, Canada M6S 2C8

Publisher: Roly Allen
Editorial Director: Zara Larcombe
Editor: Francesca Leung
Managing Specialist Editor: Frank Gallaugher
Editor: Rachel Silverlight
Admin Assistant: Sarah Vaughan
Art Director: Julie Weir
Designer: Sarah Strandoo
Production Controller: Marina Maher

ISBN 978-1-78157-827-8

A CIP catalogue record for this book is available from the British Library.

Printed and bound in China

10 9 8 7 6 5 4 3 2

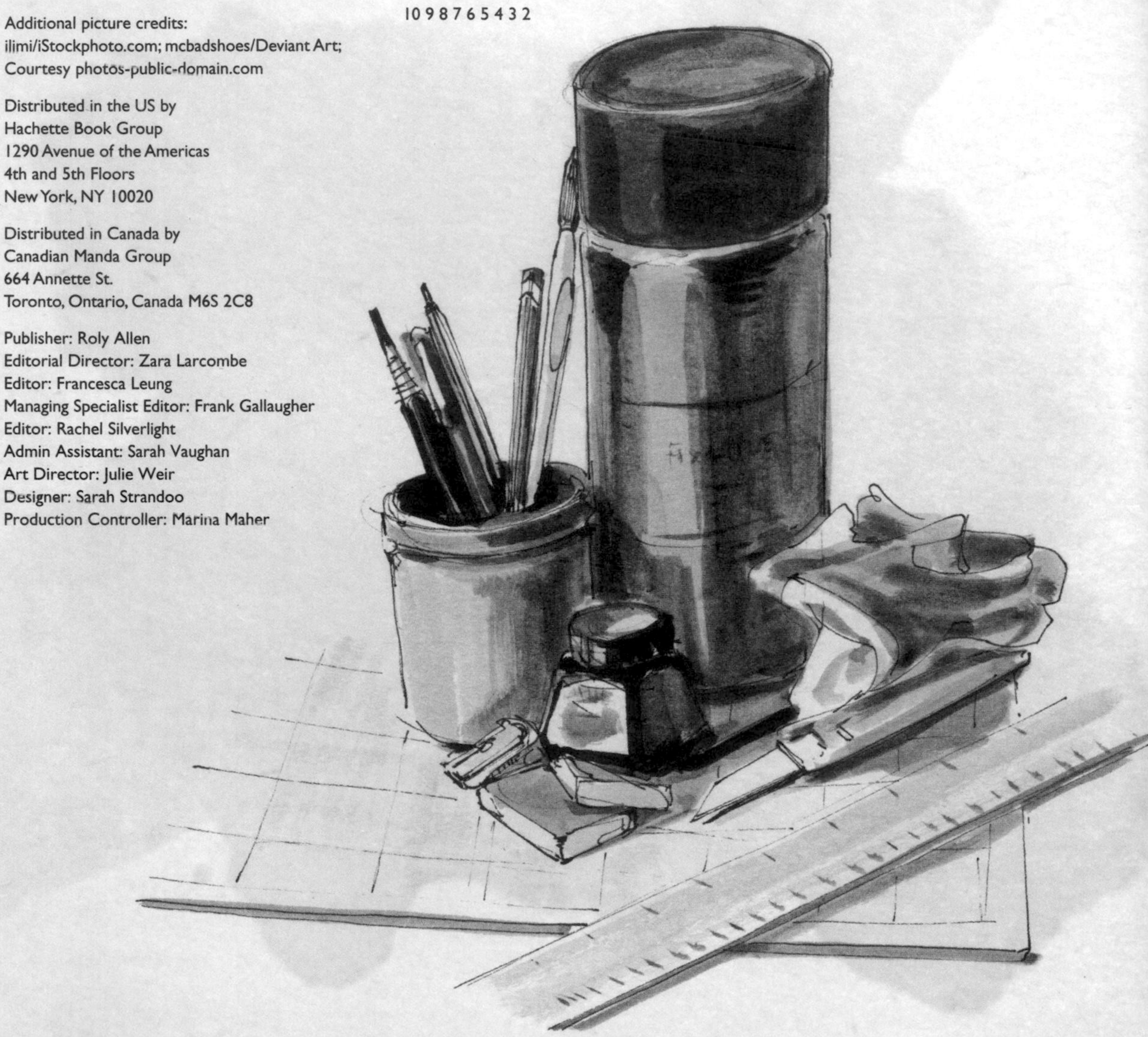

YOU WILL BE ABLE TO DRAW BY THE END OF THIS BOOK.

JAKE SPICER

ilex

IN THIS SKETCHBOOK

06

WHAT DO YOU WANT TO DRAW TODAY?

16

PART 01: SEEING

62

PART 02: FEELING

112

PART 03: KNOWING

140

PART 04: SELECTING

156

WHAT'S NEXT?

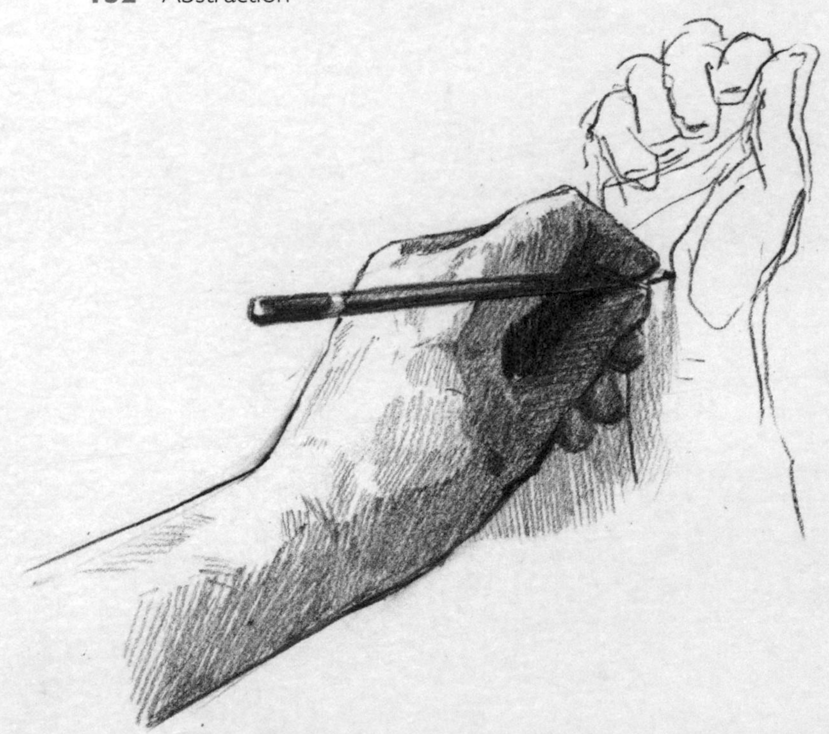

WHAT DO YOU WANT TO DRAW TODAY?

TIME

WARM-UP EXERCISES

AROUND 15 MINUTES

LONG DRAWING EXERCISES

LOCATION

AT HOME

ON PUBLIC TRANSPORT

LOCATION CONTINUED

IN THE COUNTRYSIDE

IN THE TOWN

GALLERIES & MUSEUMS

IN A LIFE-DRAWING CLASS

SUBJECTS

PEOPLE

FABRIC

ANIMALS

LANDSCAPE

BUILDINGS

STILL LIFE

INTRODUCTION

This book is for anybody who wants to draw more, whether you are learning from scratch or developing existing skills. When you're learning to draw, the most important book you'll own is a sketchbook, and this is a sketchbook with training wheels. It contains practical advice, words of encouragement, and plenty of blank pages to fill in yourself. If you work through each chapter from beginning to end, drawing as you go, then by the end of this book you will be able to draw.

LEARNING TO DRAW

The thing is, you already can draw. As children we all draw and paint but, as we get older, writing takes precedence and we stop drawing regularly. Drawing is a skill that develops with practice, just like playing a musical instrument. The more you draw the better you'll get; everybody can learn to draw well and regular practice will take you farther than innate talent alone. It is not that some people can draw effortlessly, while others find it difficult; at the beginning we all struggle. The key is to enjoy the process of learning. It might take a long time to reach your initial goals and, by the time you get there, your intentions will most likely have changed. You might find that as you draw you are held back by a critical internal voice; take its criticisms and lay them aside. Be kind to yourself as you develop, recognize the progress you make at each stage, and enjoy the journey of learning to draw.

DRAWING AS A PROCESS

Drawing is curiosity made tangible, and it begins with seeing. By drawing more, you learn to look at familiar things through new eyes; the process of drawing becomes an excuse to stare long and hard at the world around you. As well as a method of picture-making, drawing is a looking tool, allowing you to focus your concentration on a small part of the world in order to capture its fugitive appearance. Even when you are drawing from your imagination, the imagery you use is plucked from remembered observations. Any single drawing can succeed or fail, so instead of judging your ability on your outcomes, work on improving your process. Aim to become better at looking, to improve the connection between your eye and hand, and to make clearer marks in response to what you see. When you are more confident in your process, you'll find you are much happier with the drawings you make.

VISUAL LANGUAGE

Drawing is a visual language, it is a way of describing observations and imaginings through meaningful marks. Drawing isn't just a means of making art, it is a means of communicating. We draw to communicate more often than we realize: drawing maps for directions, sketching new layouts of furniture in a room, or making pictures for signage. It is also a way of bringing ideas that we don't yet have the words for to life; almost every man-made thing around you began its life as a sketch on a designer's drawing board. Just like when you are learning a new language, your drawings will be clumsy at first, and you'll rely on borrowed marks and techniques, as you might use stock phrases in a foreign tongue. As you learn the essential grammar of drawing, you'll become clearer in your visual articulation and more poetic in the drawn marks you make.

QUALITY

There is no right or wrong way to draw, but there are better and worse ways of getting what you want from a drawing. The success of a drawing depends on its intention, so it is difficult to talk about good drawings and bad drawings without context. When you start a drawing, know why you are making it; you might be trying to practice your looking or mark-making, to record something you've seen, or to communicate an idea. At first, keep all of the drawings you make; the ones you deem to contain the most mistakes will be the ones you learn most from.

STYLE

A consistent style is elusive and, as you are developing, your drawings will seem especially erratic. The recognizable style of an established artist is the result of personal vision and marks made with specific materials, consistently applied to a particular subject and carefully selected for presentation. Allow your own style to evolve naturally; you'll often find that others can perceive your style of working more easily than you can.

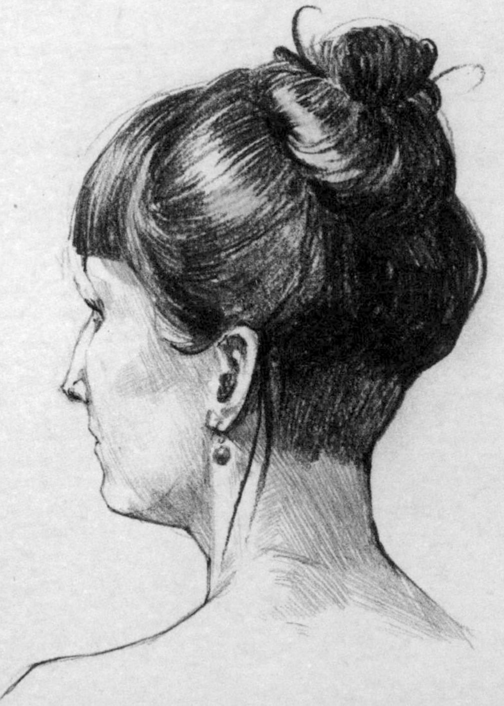

WHAT YOU NEED...

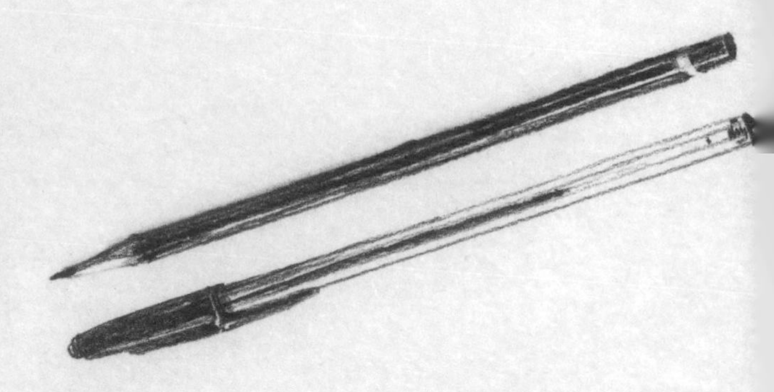

TIME

In order to learn to draw, you need to make time to draw. It takes as long to finish a quick drawing as it does to deliberate over whether or not to get out your sketchbook. Make time in your week to sit down and draw without distraction or interruption, as well as taking advantage of the many brief opportunities you might have to sketch during your day.

PENCILS

The graphite pencil is a staple drawing medium; it is inexpensive, portable, and capable of a wide range of marks. Although a 2B pencil will be enough for this book, three grades of hardness will allow you greater flexibility: an H for hard edges and pale grays, a 2B for general sketching, and a 6B for your darkest tones. Vary your pressure and scribble dark to light to test your pencils below.

BALLPOINT PENS

The humble ballpoint is a versatile and inherently linear drawing tool, the marks it makes varying with pressure. The impossibility of erasure and disposable feel of the pen encourage playful and unselfconscious mark-making. Carry several in case one runs dry and scribble in the margins to test them.

SCRIBBLE HERE

HARD, PALE

9H
8H
7H
6H
5H
4H
3H
2H
H
HB
B
2B
3B
4B
5B
6B
7B
8B
9B

SOFT, BLACK, DARK

TIPS FOR SETTING UP TO DRAW

- You might stand to draw in a museum, or across a crowded market place. Find something to lean against to keep you stable.
- If you're fortunate enough to find a chair or a sofa to sit on as you sketch, use your leg to angle your book towards you.
- When you are drawing at a table, avoid working flat as it can distort your drawing and hurt your back. Use a board to support your sketchbook, angled between your lap and the table edge.

USING THIS BOOK

This is a book to draw in, to fill with notes, and make your own.

USE THE MARGINS TO WRITE EXTRA NOTES

You can get started with just a pen or pencil and, as you go through the book, new materials will be introduced, all of which are listed on page 158. Although the book could be read in a weekend, there is no need to hurry to complete it. To really make the most of the exercises, you should try them first here, then practice them again in a second sketchbook, working through them in your own time before moving on to the next exercise. Make notes on the exercises, cross out things you didn't get on with, and add your own ideas as notes. Learning to draw is a long and personal journey—this book can serve as both guidebook and diary on that road. On the opposite page is some useful advice to bear in mind.

1.

tart at the beginning
he initial exercises will elp you develop skills that ou'll be able to use later in he book. One lesson builds n another.

2.

Draw in this book
This book has blank pages to draw in, use them and don't be afraid of filling them. This is a book to help you learn and it is just for you.

3.

Get a second sketchbook
Get yourself a blank sketchbook in which to repeat the exercises and use it to develop your own ideas.

4.

Repeat what you enjoy
When you find an exercise you enjoy or find useful, practice it and repeat regularly.

ADD YOUR OWN ANNOTATIONS TO THE PAGES

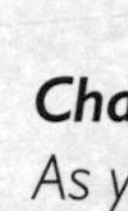

5.

Challenge yourself
As you become more confident, explore new materials and unfamiliar subjects.

6.

Use the index
Once you've worked through the book, use it as an exercise book that you can return to for ideas and inspirations, pages 6–9 will help you find exercises appropriate for where you are, how much time you have, and what you want to learn.

7.

Commit to your drawing
Draw with intention and purpose, don't hurry through the book unnecessarily.

8.

Make many drawings
You'll need to make many bad drawings in order to make ones you are happy with.

9.

Make drawing a part of your life
Find ways to draw as part of your day.

PART 01

SEEING

Drawing begins with looking. Even imaginative drawings are rooted in the memories of things that you once observed. For the moment, you'll need to let go of your preconceptions of how the world looks and begin to see everything around you through fresh eyes. The aim is to learn to draw what you see intuitively, simply looking and making marks without the critical internal voice of your intellect holding you back.

SKILLS OF PERCEPTION

This section is about developing core skills that you could use to draw anything that you can see, from hands to horses and seascapes to cities. The exercises here can be applied to drawing anything—don't feel restricted to the subject suggested. The more you practice the exercises, the easier you will find them. Musicians practice their scales, runners do laps of a track, and you will need to draw from observation.

1. EDGES & LINES

Lines are fundamental units of drawing, and are often the first marks you'll lay down on your page to make sense of a subject. Lines often stand in for edges, boundaries between the subject and its surroundings, or between areas of light and dark. Linear drawings are inherently stylized, they are simplifications of what we see; a visual impression reduced down to a few marks. Look up from this book and trace your eye around the things you see in front of you—it is these edges that lines want to stick to.

2. SHAPES & SPACES

Join up several lines and you have a shape. When you translate the three-dimensional world into a two-dimensional drawing all of the shapes you draw should fit together like the pieces of a jigsaw puzzle. In order to see the world as it is—rather than as you expect it to be —you'll need your eye to sharply perceive shapes. A person looks like a person, so when you go to draw somebody you'll be hampered by your idea of how a person should look. By drawing all of the visual shapes that make up and surround your subject, you'll find it easier to draw the particular example that is in front of you.

3. TONE & COLOR

We see the world through the reflection of light; we see light and dark, and we see color. We'll leave color alone for now. Look up from the book again. Imagine the view in front of you as a black and white photograph—take a photograph if you can. Very little of what you'll see is truly black and very little truly white, most of what you see will be gray, from fresh, pale grays, full of light, to deep, velvety grays that border on black. If your aim is to draw a convincing illusion of what you see then it is this range of gray tones that you'll need to capture. Where lines and shapes help you structure your observations, it is the tonal values of light and dark that will add depth and form to your drawing.

1.
2.
3.

PART 01: SEEING

LINE – MARK-MAKING

LINE

Whether your lines are hard or delicate, playful or precise, make them confidently. Let your pencil or pen rest in your fingers comfortably and draw as if it were an extension of your hand; explore the kind of lines that your medium likes to make. Draw lines slow and fast, make short sharp marks from your fingers and arcing marks from your wrist. Practice drawing lines on the opposite page.

RACTICE
ERE

PART 01: SEEING

BLIND CONTOURS – EXERCISE

WHAT YOU NEED

- 1–5 minutes
- Ballpoint pen or pencil
- Any subject

Some drawing exercises help you practice a process, not just achieve an outcome. This exercise will help you observe your subject intently, see edges clearly, and draw with a single, unselfconscious line. It is a playful, meditative exercise that makes a good warm-up to a session of more conventional drawing.

Your subject could be a person on a train, a bedroom interior, a vase of flowers—anything. Set a timer, or draw for the length of a song. Rest your eye on your subject as if the point of your focus was your pen-tip. Without looking down, touch your pen to the blank page. Slowly trace your eye over the edges of your subject and, as you do, let your pen trace the journey of your eye on the page. Don't look at the page at all, but keep your eye firmly fixed on your subject, drawing with a continuous flowing line. When the time is up take your pen off the paper and look at your drawing for the first time. It will inevitably look peculiar and out of proportion, but it will be made with a confident flowing mark—the result of hard observation.

RACTICE
ERE

PART 01: SEEING

EDGES & RELATIONSHIPS

Making a line drawing is like doing a dot-to-dot where you have to draw the dots yourself.

As you trace the edges of your subject, you are navigating the spaces between points—accurately judging the relationships between those points will help you establish accurate proportions. As you draw, your eyes should be constantly flitting between paper and subject, continuously comparing the two like a spot-the-difference puzzle. The more time you spend looking at your subject, the more answers you will find to the questions your drawing creates.

DOT-TO-DOT

Quickly dashed marks can help you to establish the overall proportions of a subject early, even if you reassess them as you draw. Start with marks for the top, bottom, left, and right extremes.

LOOK, HOLD, DRAW

Look first, then draw. Look hard at your subject; find the edge you want to draw. See where it starts, see where it finishes, and the rhythm of the line between those points. See the edge, hold it in your memory for a moment, then draw it.

REHEARSE A MARK

Overdrawing heavy marks on a page can obscure the final line you settle on; don't make more lines than you have to. If you need to let your hand rehearse a line, use loose, light marks, *pentimenti*, that feel their way across a space as your eye darts from subject to paper. Then draw in a single, confident final stroke that pins that line in place.

EDGE OF THE ROOM – EXERCISE

WHAT YOU NEED

- 5–30 minutes
- Ballpoint pen or pencil
- Any interior space

Man-made spaces are full of edges; offices, museums, and train carriages are filled with human paraphernalia that afford clear outlines for our eyes to find. This exercise builds on the last, using a continuous line to trace your eye's journey around a room. This time you can look back at the page as you draw.

Find an interesting corner of detail in the room you are in. Start your drawing somewhere near the middle of a double spread (overleaf). Touch pen to paper and with a single, continuous line trace the edges of the objects in front of you.

Move out from your starting point along any edges you see and keep your eyes constantly flitting from page to room, up and down, drawing all the time and never stopping to erase anything. The drawing will inevitably fall out of proportion —that is ok. Draw until you have filled the spread. This is an exercise you could try daily, to record the spaces you visit. It can be picked up in a moment and applied to any interior. There is something particularly attractive about a whole sketchbook filled with unself-conscious little line drawings of rooms.

PRACTICE
HERE

PART 01: SEEING

SHAPE & SPACE

Objectivity is the key to making clear observations. When you stop seeing a cup as a cup and you learn to see it simply as a shape in space, you'll find it much easier to draw.

By practicing exercises that focus on the negative spaces around your subject, you can train your eyes to see the shapes of spaces more easily. As you build your toolbox of perceptual skills, you'll find different ways to solve problems in your drawings.

BIG SHAPES TO SMALL

Working from one small area of detail to another makes it easy to fall out of proportion as you draw. Get the overall shape of your subject drawn in early, then refine your drawing, finding increasingly smaller shapes within that space.

DRAW TRAPPED SHAPES

When you see a negative space bounded on all sides by your subject, draw that trapped shape exactly as you see it—you will bring fewer preconceptions to that space than you do to the subject. If it doesn't fit with the subject as you've drawn it, reassess your drawing.

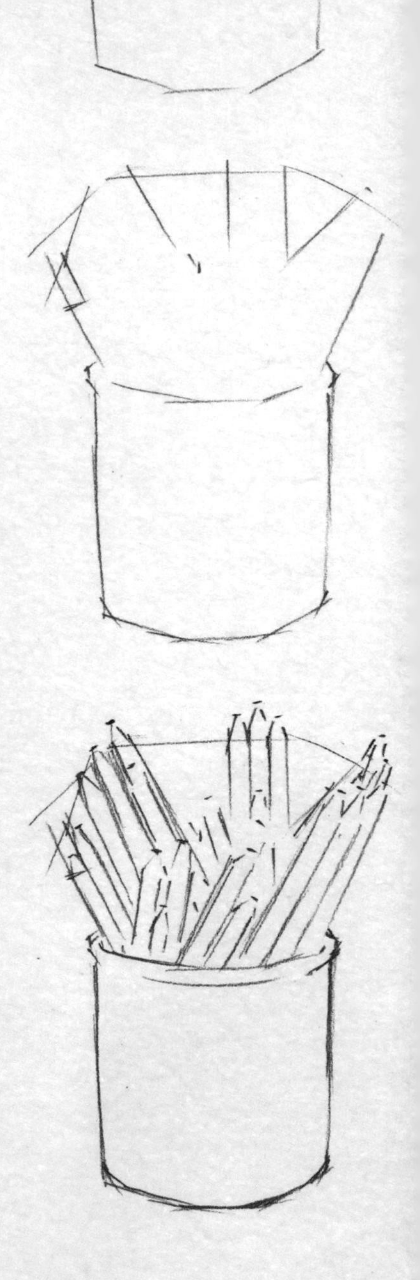

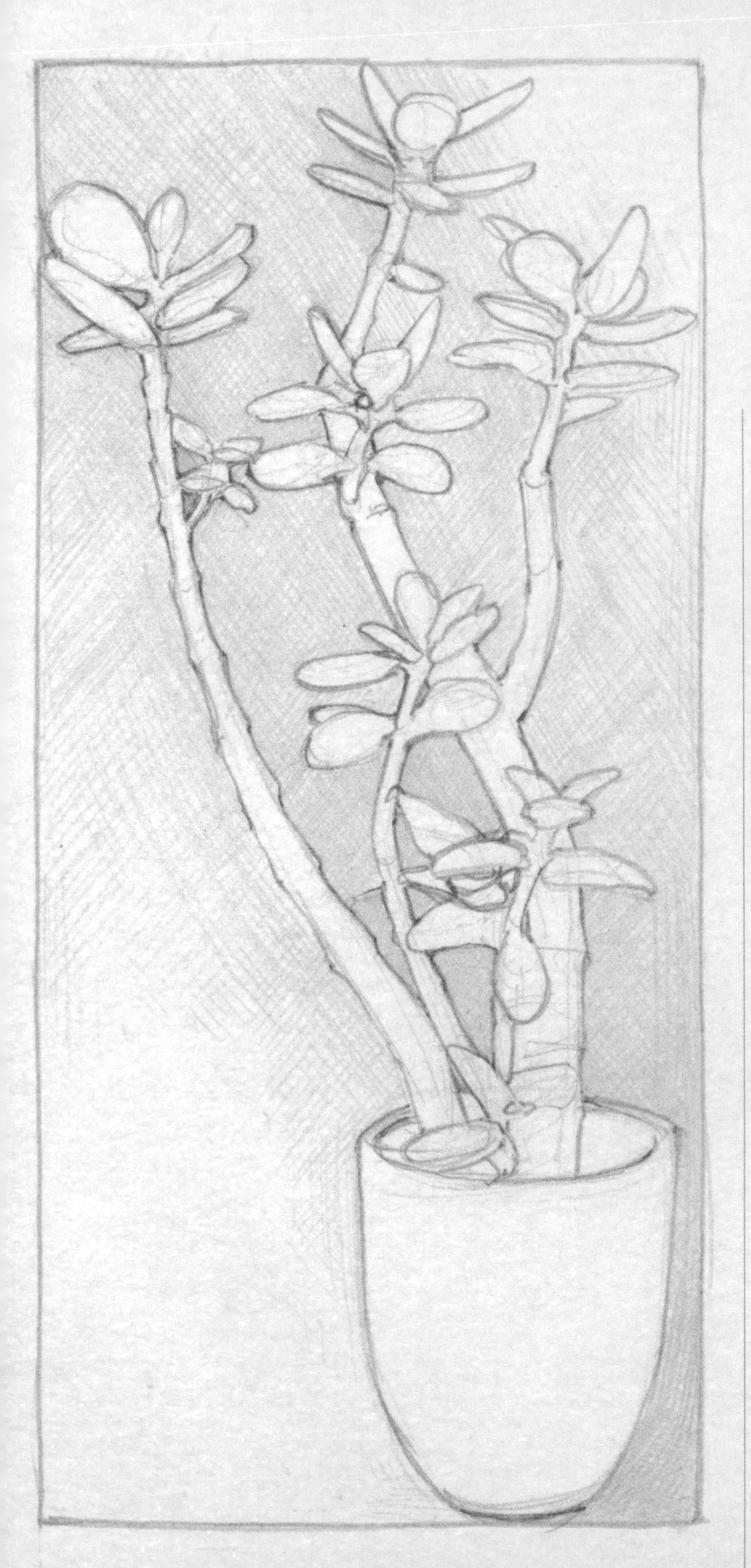

CREATE BOUNDARIES

Trapped shapes can be easy to see, but the negative space around your subject has no clear boundary. Imagine a box around your subject to help you see the surrounding negative spaces. You can use a viewfinder to help you—take a look at the next page.

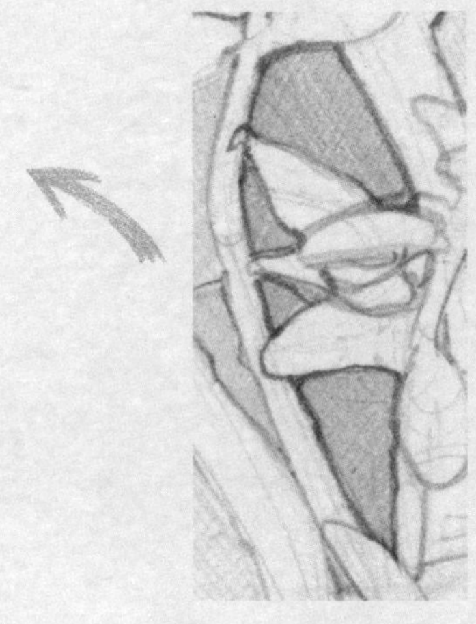

PART 01: SEEING

VIEWFINDERS - MATERIALS

A sketchbook page has boundaries where the visual world doesn't. A viewfinder will help you to put edges around what you see. Like any perceptual aids, viewfinders are best used sparingly so you don't become overly reliant on them.

MAKING A VIEWFINDER

Find some stiff card to make a viewfinder and cut it to the size of this page. Cereal package cardboard, mountboard, or sketchbook backing works well. You'll also need a craft knife, a pencil, a steel rule, and a cutting mat.

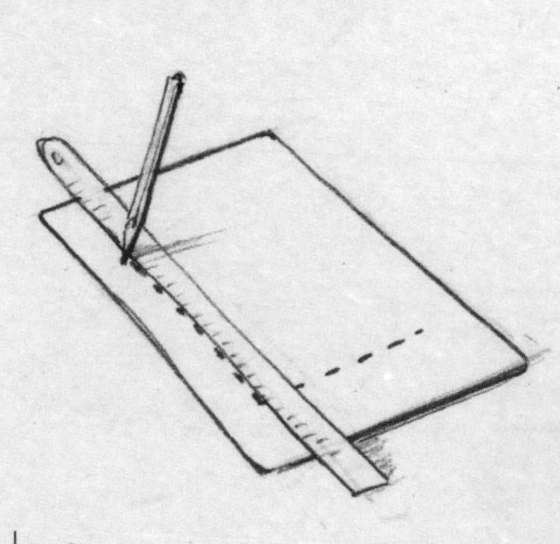

1.

Draw out an aperture with the pencil and ruler.

2.

Using the steel rule and mat for safety, cut out the aperture

3.

Don't throw it away!

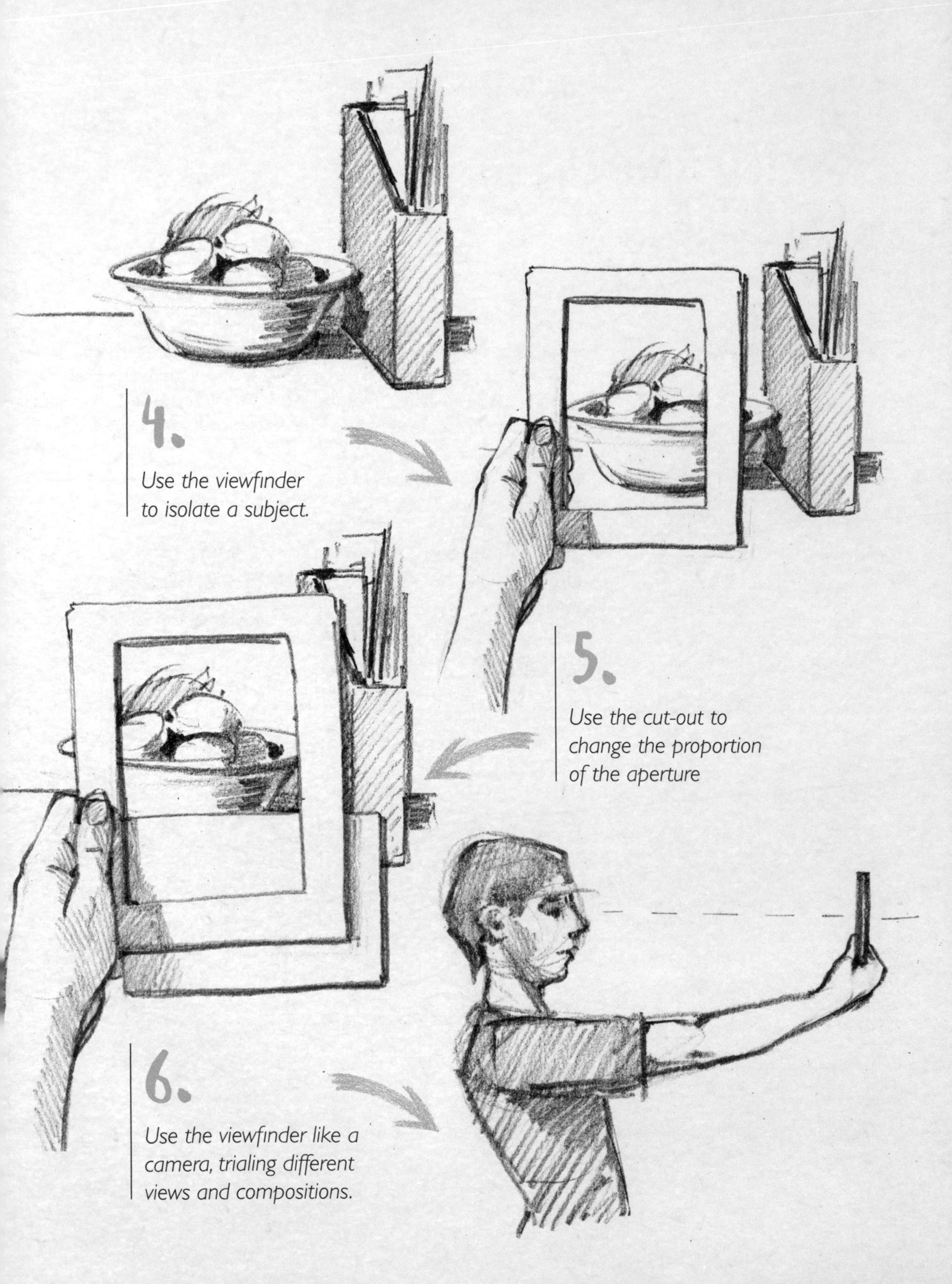
4.
Use the viewfinder to isolate a subject.
5.
Use the cut-out to change the proportion of the aperture
6.
Use the viewfinder like a camera, trialing different views and compositions.

PART 01: SEEING

TRAPPED SHAPES – EXERCISE

WHAT YOU NEED

- 15–30 minutes
- A chair or stool
- Pencil, eraser & viewfinder

Bring your perceptual skills into play to draw a familiar, but complex subject. You can use a viewfinder for this exercise, but it isn't obligatory. As well as a chair, this works well with trees, flowers, or with a model in a life-drawing class.

Use the viewfinder to create boundaries to work within, draw the big shapes of the chair, find trapped shapes, and elaborate on the drawing.

PRACTICE
HERE

PART 01: SEEING

TONE

Where a vocabulary of linear marks can describe the edges and shapes of objects, tonal marks give those shapes form.

A line is an imaginary imposition and often stands in for a boundary, where tone represents the world as it is seen: edges of light against edges of dark with no line in between. How you choose to balance line and tone in a drawing is your own decision.

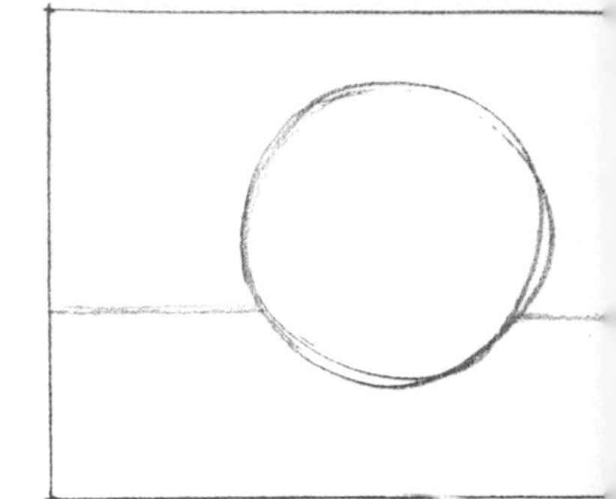

CHIAROSCURO

A circle is a flat shape. For that flat shape to appear spherical on a flat page its surface needs to be rendered with tone. The edges of cast shadows and gradations of light can be suggested with initial lines. Simple, parallel marks can be used to sketch tone fast. Gradated tone in the background creates contrast at the edges of the circle, helping it to stand out on the page.

TRY IT HERE

TONAL SHAPES

Shadows have shapes; sometimes sharp edged, sometimes soft. Look at the shapes of the shadows you can see and define them clearly in your drawings. Squinting or unfocusing your eyes can help you to see them better.

VALUE

Separating the complex visual world into a manageable range of tones can help you to see shapes of shadow more clearly. The very lightest lights and darkest darks occur much less frequently than you might expect.

PART 01: SEEING

VALUES – MARK-MAKING

VALUES

Explore different ways of making tonal marks and fill in the blank spaces with a variety of tones. Try this exercise with each new material you try.

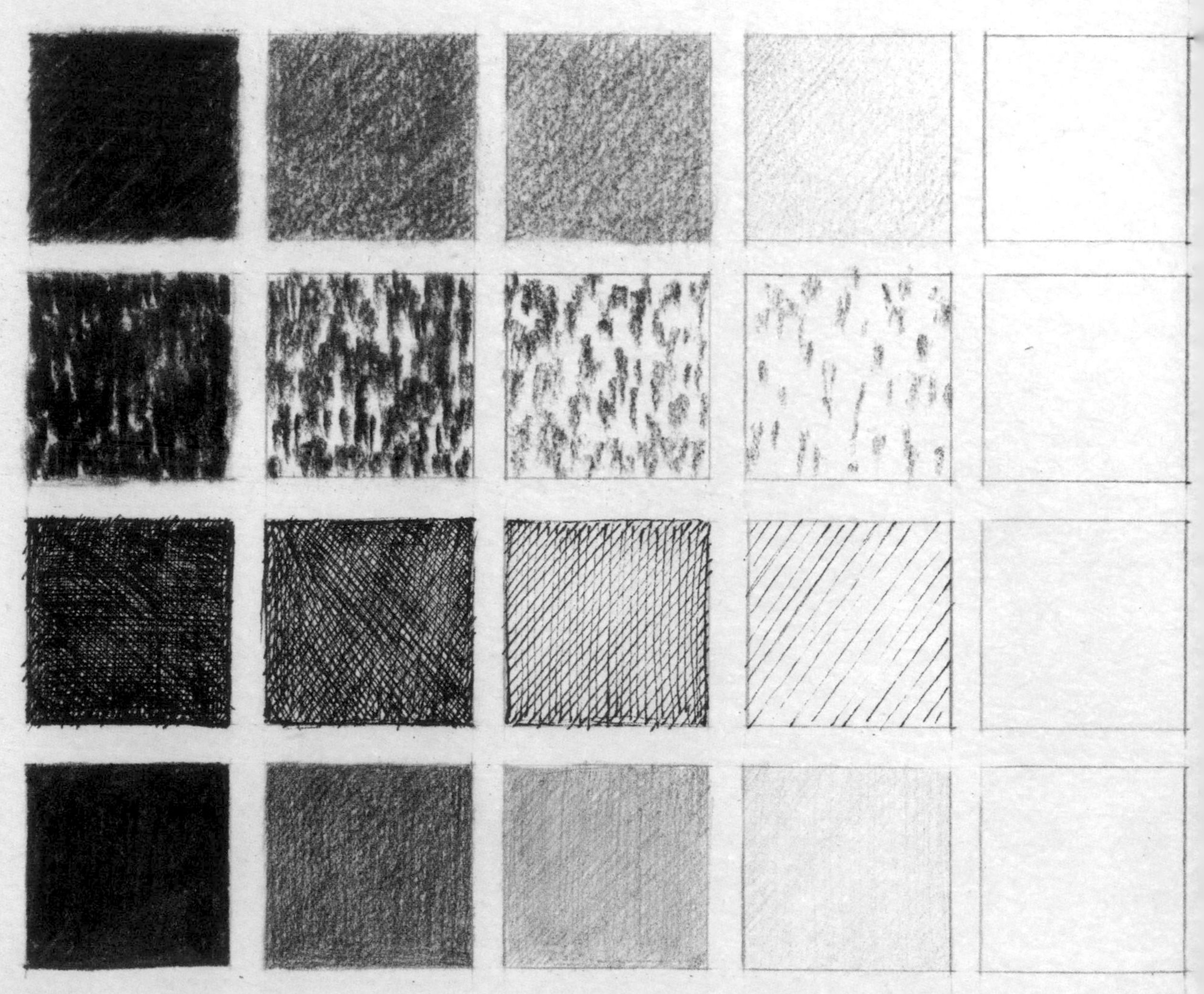

PRACTICE
HERE

PART 01: SEEING

THE HAND THAT SEES – EXERCISE

WHAT YOU NEED

- 10–30 minutes
- A 2B pencil
- Any view

The pressure placed on your pencil to create different tones should eventually become an instinctive reaction to the values that your eye has perceived. In this exercise you'll free yourself from line, scanning your eyes over the room around you and drawing with a continuous, controlled scribble.

Treat the view ahead of you as your subject, whether you are indoors, outdoors, or looking out of the window. Settle down comfortably with a sharp pencil and practice a few scribbles in the margins. Start in the top corner of the double spread overleaf and draw what you see with a controlled scribble, without sketching in any initial lines. Press harder for darks, softer for lights; feel your way across the page until you have filled it with tone. Your eyes should be a scanner, your hand a printer.

PRACTICE
HERE

CHARCOAL – MATERIALS

The next few exercises use charcoal. It is a wonderful medium for making tonal drawings, but a tricky one to use in sketchbooks; you could use a soft graphite pencil as an alternative.

Charcoal is black, velvety and smudges easily. Its disadvantages are also its strengths—it is easily erased and can be moved around with a finger, cloth, or tightly rolled paper called a tortillion.

Willow charcoal comes in round sticks, it is cheap, ubiquitous, and smudges easily. Vine charcoal is often cut square; it is harder and can be sanded to a point for fine detail. Compressed charcoal sticks contain a binder and give a very dense black. Charcoal pencils use compressed charcoal, can be sharpened and vary in texture and quality.

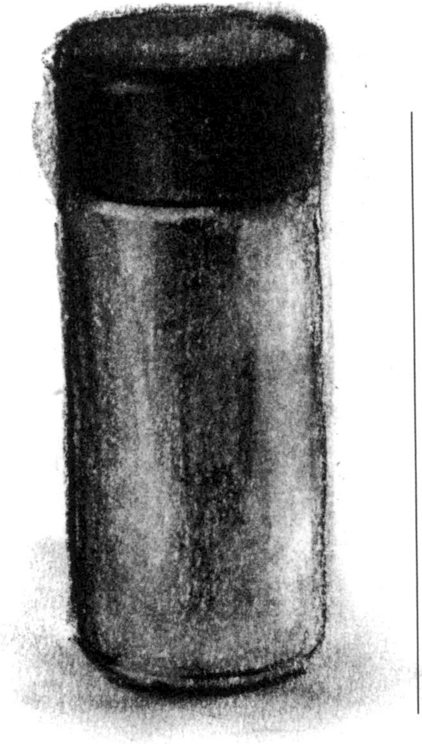

USE IN SKETCHBOOKS

Charcoal needs to be sprayed with a fixative to stop it smudging; spray the fixative evenly from an arm's length away. Specially formulated artist's fixative is ideal—some people use hairspray, but this can yellow a drawing over time. No matter how well fixed it is, a little charcoal will always transfer onto the opposite page of a sketchbook, so you should draw on one page, leaving the other blank, or slip a piece of paper between a double spread to minimize the harm to your drawing. There can however be something peculiarly attractive about the ghost of a drawing left on the opposite page.

TEST YOUR CHARCOAL HERE AND SEE HOW MUCH RUBS OFF ONTO THE OPPOSITE PAGE

SUBTRACTIVE TONE – MARK-MAKING

An eraser is a valuable drawing tool that draws light back into dark. Scrub some charcoal onto the page opposite and use a piece of cloth or tissue to rub the charcoal into the surface until it is a midtone gray. Use a sharp-edged eraser to draw light into the midtone, or darken it with more charcoal. Fix it when you are finished. The same principle can be applied to graphite.

RACTICE
ERE

SEA SHADOWS – EXERCISE

WHAT YOU NEED

- 10–30 minutes
- Charcoal, cloth & eraser
- A landscape or seascape

Drawings don't always need to begin with lines. A camera captures fleeting light effects in a moment, but a drawing happens over time; the advantage of this is that you can consider and experience your environment, capturing several moments in time in a single image. A subtractive charcoal drawing allows you to draw sweeping masses of dark and quickly erase shapes of light to capture the shifting light on a landscape or the repeating rhythms of the sea.

Sit in the landscape and think about what you'd like to capture about the scene; consider the atmosphere of your drawing as much as its composition. Turn two pages ahead and scrub one page with charcoal, rubbing it back to a midtone with a cloth and leaving the other page blank. Erase patches of light away; draw in hard edges with more charcoal. When a fleeting effect of light strikes the landscape, hold it in your mind as you erase or add charcoal to capture it. The same exercise can easily be applied to figures, interiors, or still life.

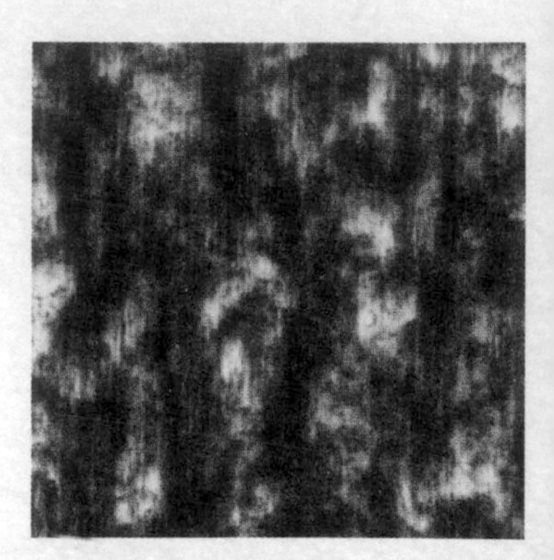

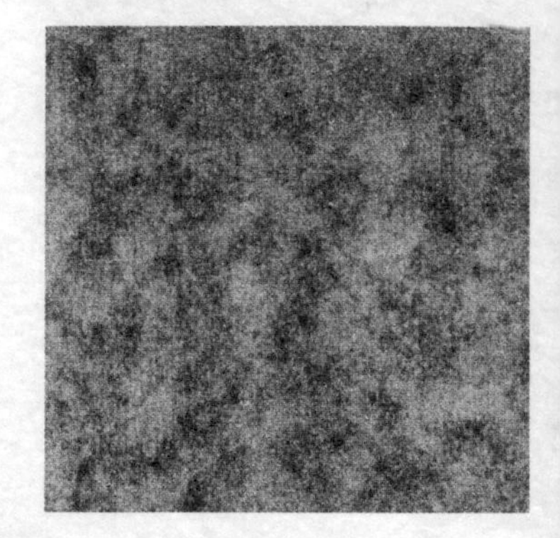

REMEMBER TO FIX YOUR
DRAWING AFTERWARDS

PRACTICE ON THE OPPOSITE PAGE
(LEAVE THIS ONE BLANK)

PART 01: SEEING

INK PENS – MATERIALS

The humble ballpoint has already been introduced, but there are many wonderful pens to draw with.

The consistent fiber-tip is beloved of urban sketchers; it comes in a variety of nib sizes. Brush pens give a wonderful variety of line. Experiment with different pens and test to see if the ink is soluble in water once it is dry on the page—if it is, you can use a brush and water to make washes and gradients.

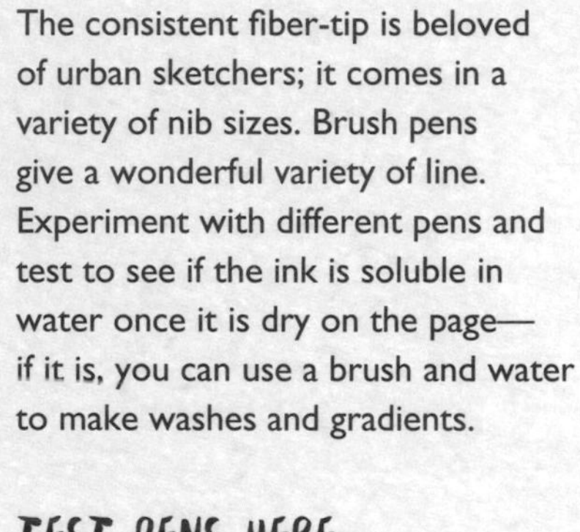

TEST PENS HERE

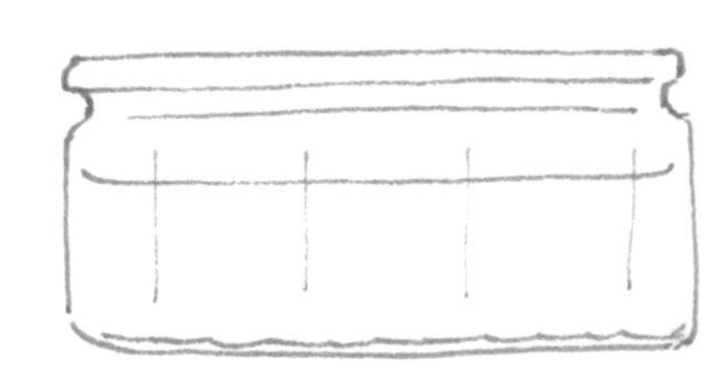

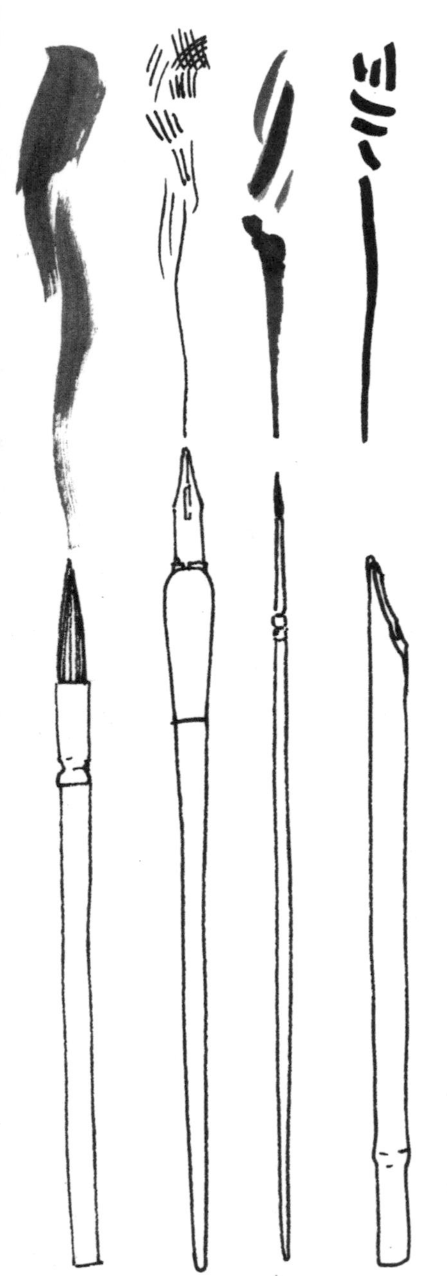

Ink can be applied directly with a variety of implements, from dip pens to brushes to twigs. Experiment with different types and make sure your ink has dried before closing your sketchbook; you'll need a pot of ink, a pot of water, and some tissue.

TEST PENS HERE

PART 01: SEEING

HATCHING -MARK-MAKING

Hatching involves building up lots of lines in parallel to establish a mass of dark tone. Cross-hatching allows you to create even darker tones through layering parallel lines in different directions. Experiment with hatching and cross-hatching in pen and pencil.

RACTICE
ERE

PART 01: SEEING

ARRANGEMENTS – EXERCISE

WHAT YOU NEED

- 15–45 minutes
- Preferred medium
- Several items on a table

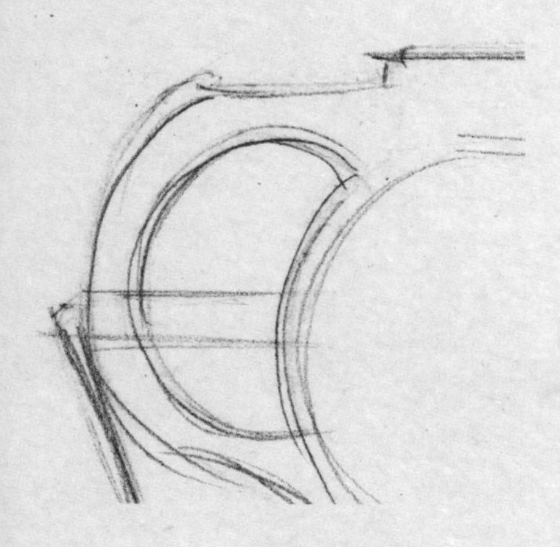

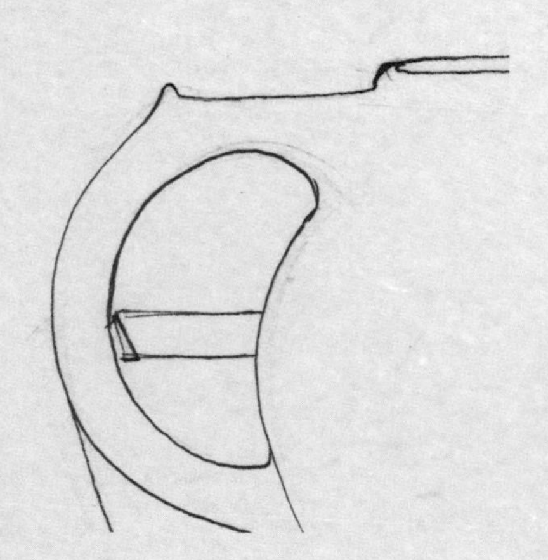

Drawing a familiar object allows you to look at it with fresh eyes, to appreciate its shape, form, and the way in which light falls on its surface. Still-life drawing can celebrate the simplicity of humble objects, glorify significant items, or gather together symbolic objects to tell a story.

Gather a few items on a table in front of you and arrange them to create an interesting composition. Move around the arrangement to select the best angle to draw from. As you sketch the objects, exercise everything you have learnt so far. Use line to make sense of your subjects' shapes—use negative spaces to check their proportions—layer on tone, using your eraser to draw in highlights. Look hard at the gathered objects—find a vocabulary of marks that suits your subject.

This drawing was made with a 0.3mm fiber-tip pen, over a pencil under-drawing.

PRACTICE
HERE

PART 02

FEELING

A drawing can do more than simply describe how a subject looks. At first it might be enough to represent the things you see in a language of linear and tonal marks, but you are not just a camera, limited to capturing light. The marks you make in your drawing can suggest texture, volume, and energy, and represent the subject perceived through all of your senses. This section of the book will help you put feeling into your drawings.

MARKS WITH MEANING

It isn't just what you say about your subject that's important, it's how you say it. The marks you make start in your body: quick gestures from your thumb and forefinger will make different marks compared to long, sweeping marks from the elbow. A mark made quickly has a different energetic quality to a mark made slowly and both have their value in drawings. A line drawn with all the weight of the body behind it is darker, and feels heavier than a pale line made with light-handed delicacy. The more you draw, the broader your repertoire of marks becomes.

MASS

Imagine an armful of fruit and vegetables, piled on a table. A line drawing would capture their shape; a tonal study could make for a satisfying illusion but there is more to the fruit and vegetables than how they look. As you draw them, remember the weight of each object as you placed it, remember how an apple felt, grasped in your hand. How could your drawing describe the mass and volume of that apple, and how its form fills a space?

ESTURE & WEIGHT

mong the nestled vegetables is spray of flowers. The vegetables ave a stoic weight as they sit on the bletop; they are hanging things, or ings from the ground, whereas the ems of the flowers suggest a thrust oward the sun, their leaves still nimated in the air. Energetic marks ade quickly from the wrist might voke the gesture of the flowers est, to contrast with the weighty oundness of the vegetables.

SURFACE

A lemon's waxy, pockmarked skin sits differently compared to the taut surface of an eggplant and the irregular mass of potatoes. It is light that helps you to see their surfaces—as you render tone in your drawing, explore how you can vary marks to make a distinction between their textures.

MASS

When you draw a person, a pot, or a tree from life you are translating something three-dimensional into a two-dimensional drawing. The outline that you might draw around them represents a horizon line; there is more on the other side. The shapes of shadow that you see simply show how a form is interrupting the path of light. The marks that you make on your page can pin down edges and shadow shapes, but they can also evoke the three-dimensional quality of your subject. Marks can talk about how an object fills a space: its volume and mass.

MARKS

Contours can show the volume of a flat shape, as they do on a map when describing the topography of a landscape. When you are drawing the surface of a curved form, think of yourself like a potter throwing a bowl on a potter's wheel; let your marks curve over the surface. Elliptical marks can suggest a convex or concave form; imagine a cross-section through your subject to give you an idea of the rhythm of curve on its surface. Vertical, horizontal, and diagonal marks can help suggest the directions of flat surfaces.

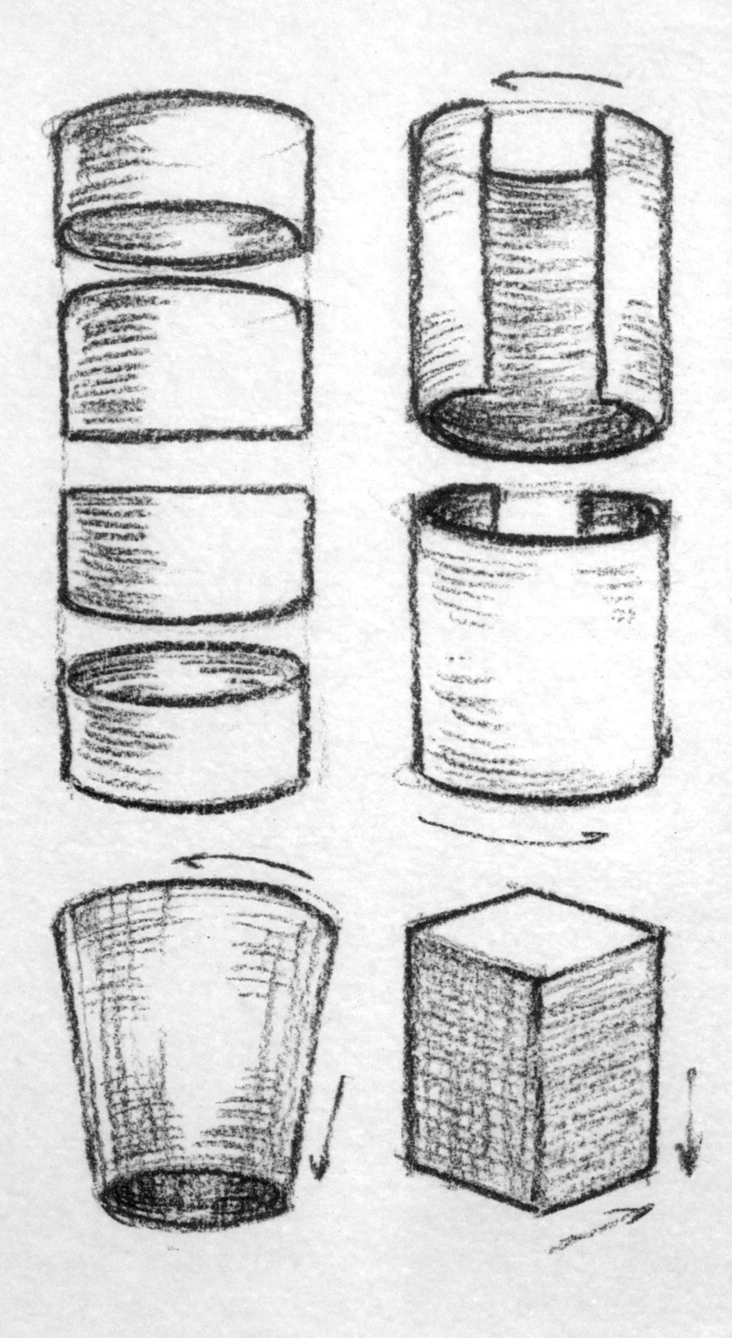

1.

In quick drawings, ellipses and spiraling marks can capture mass without relying on an outline.

2.

A line drawing is a simplification and won't always say enough about your subject: a few marks to indicate surface direction say much more.

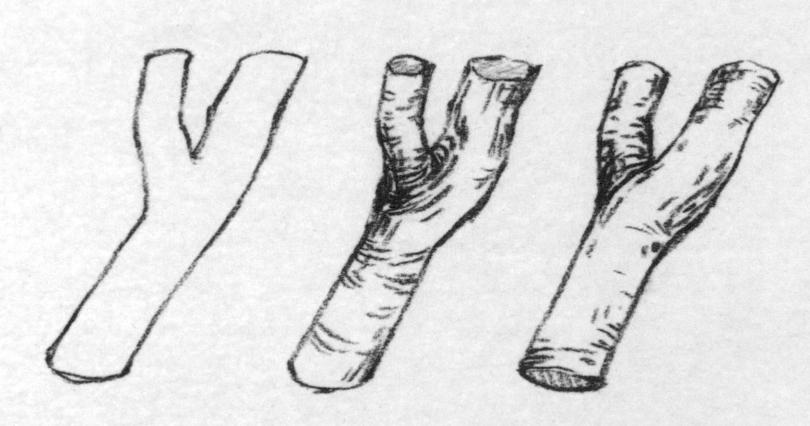

3.

A build-up of contours becomes inherently tonal, and contours can double as hatching to suggest the play of light on a form.

PART 02: FEELING

CONTOUR -MARK-MAKING

CONTOUR

Practice quick, fluid ellipses; use braceleting contours to turn a flat shape into a curved form. Bring imaginary pots into being with your marks.

RACTICE
ERE

PART 02: FEELING

POTTER'S FORMS – EXERCISE

WHAT YOU NEED

- 15 minutes–1 hour
- A charcoal or graphite pencil
- Cups, bowls, plates & pans

Stacked plates, pots, and bowls make a nest of elliptical forms. This exercise is a way to avoid the washing up by making it your subject and studying collected shapes of jumbled crockery. Keep your wrist loose as you draw and rehearse elliptical marks in the air before you touch pencil to paper, avoiding hard-edged outlines to capture the curved surfaces in front of you.

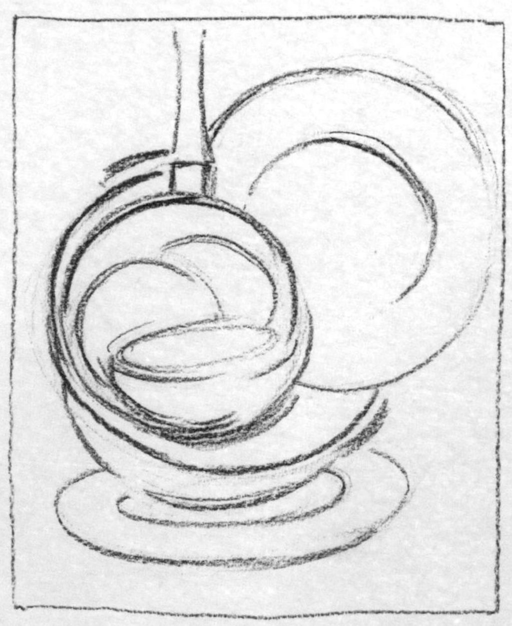

PRACTICE
HERE

PART 02: FEELING

GESTURE

If drawings focusing on mass speak about the subject as an object in space—"what it is"—then gesture drawings evoke the dynamics of the subject—"what it is doing." As you draw, you can translate the energy you perceive in your subject into marks on the page through the physical gestures you make.

GESTURAL MARK-MAKING

The marks that you make can give a feeling of tension, dynamism, or stillness. The speed at which you make the mark and variety of width and tone within a single mark will suggest gestural qualities in the subject.

FLEETING EDGES

The gesture of a speedily made mark will be preserved inherently in the varied and fluid line. If you are drawing a moving subject, you have to look hard, holding edges in your memory as you lay down marks quickly and intuitively.

CHARTING MOVEMENT

Of course you aren't limited to just drawing the subject, you can also draw its path through space to capture the sweep of an energetic gesture.

PART 02: FEELING

QUALITY OF LINE – MARK-MAKING

The way in which you make a mark affects how it appears. Explore different ways to hold your drawing tools, or use your non-drawing hand. Having less control over your material can help you make a freer, less self-conscious drawing. Make a series of continuous line drawings (see page 24), changing how you hold your pencil each time.

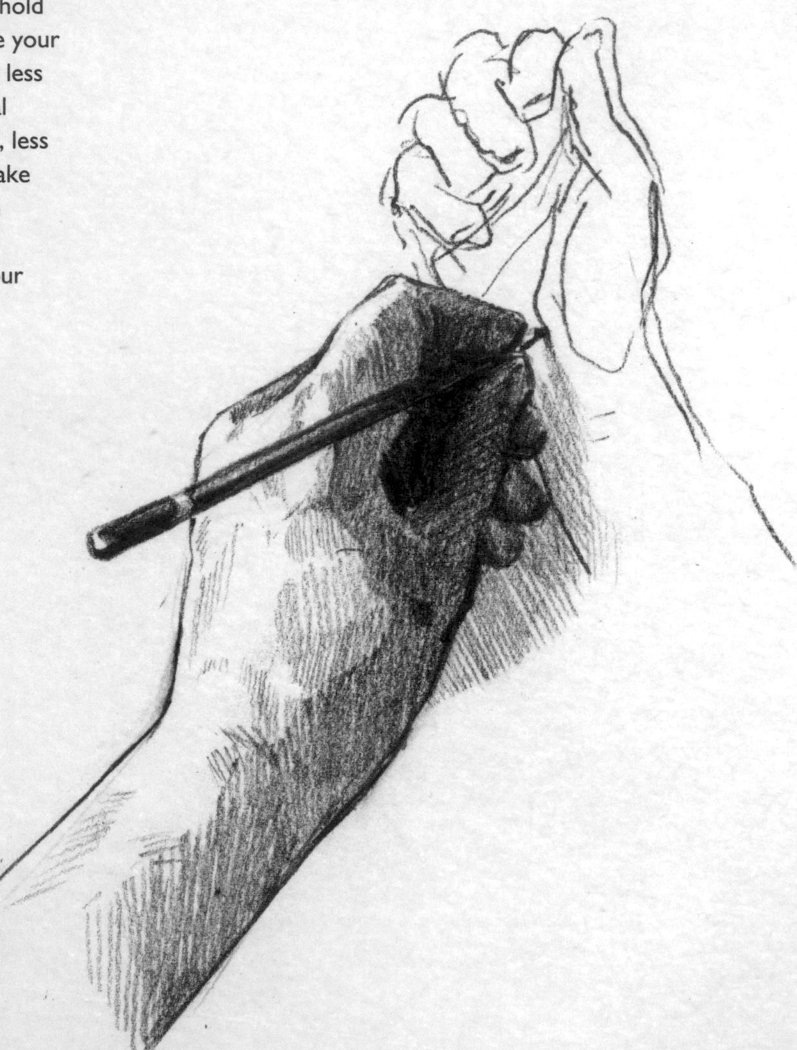

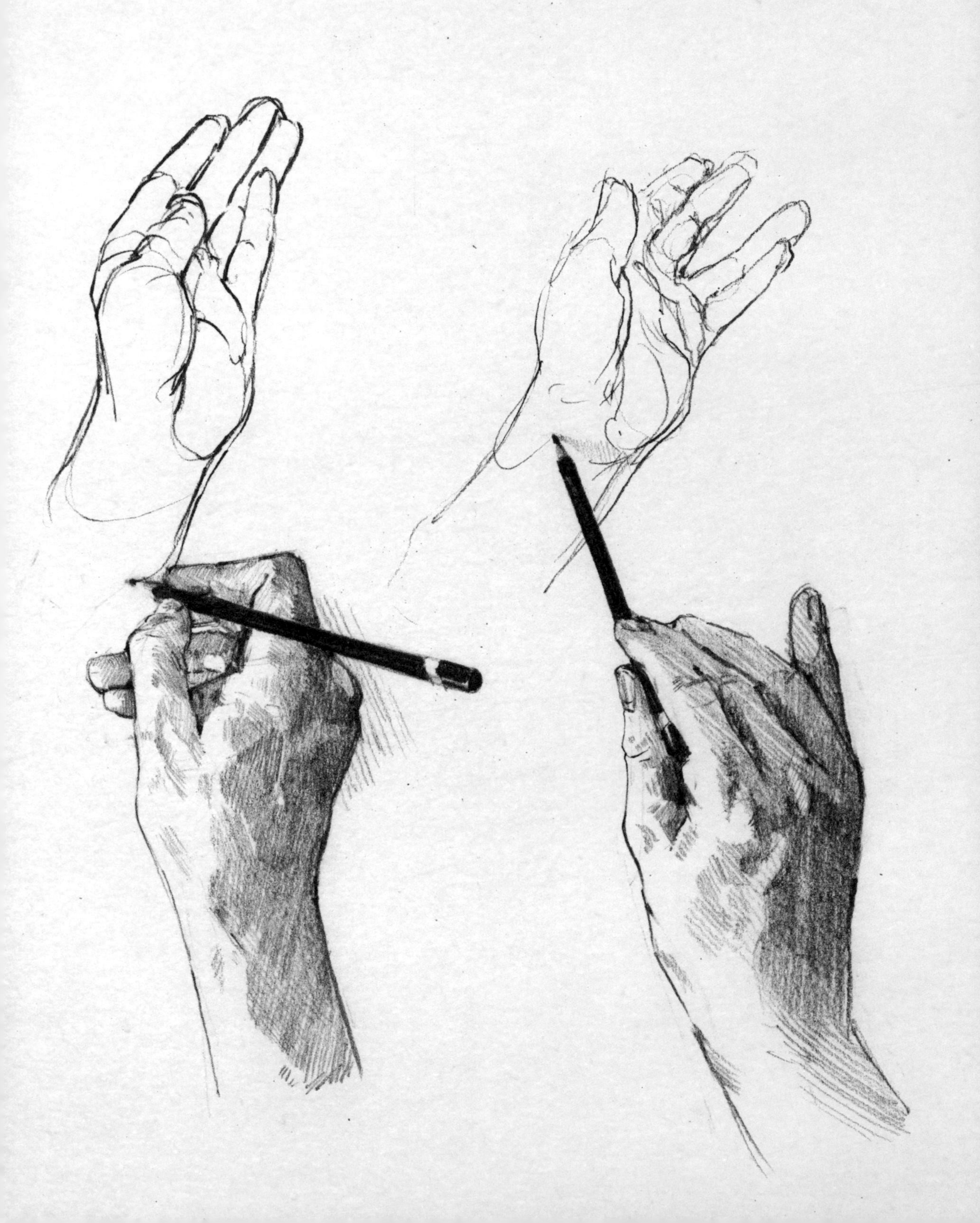

PRACTICE
HERE

PART 02: FEELING

GESTURAL TONE - EXERCISE

WHAT YOU NEED

- 1–5 minutes per sketch
- Pencil, charcoal, or ink
- A figure

Capturing a gesture can require you to see the subject as a whole before recording particular edges. This exercise works well in a life-drawing class, or when sketching moving figures on the street or on TV. You'll need to hold shapes and edges in your visual memory for fleeting moments as you draw; express the energy of the figure without getting caught up in details.

Start with a material that makes broad marks—the side of a piece of charcoal, a gray brush pen, diluted ink, or the side of a pencil—and capture the main big shapes of your subject. Use a dark, linear medium like a charcoal pencil, pen, or pencil tip to sketch in loose lines to hold the general shapes together. Finish off with a few key shadow shapes.

PRACTICE
HERE

PART 02: FEELING

CHASING TAILS – EXERCISE

WHAT YOU NEED

- 45 minutes
- A ballpoint pen
- An animal

Drawn studies are just that: a way of studying a subject. When you use drawing as a way of looking you don't always need to make a complete, polished drawing and, when you are drawing animals from life, they are unlikely to stay still long enough for a sustained drawing anyway!

This exercise works well in a zoo or an aquarium, or at home with your pets. Drawing in pen reduces the temptation to erase your drawings. Simply set up in front of your subject and try to capture their poses in lots of small sketches. You'll find you develop a page full of half-finished figures and body parts; when your subject returns to a pose similar to one in a drawing you began but abandoned, return to that earlier drawing. Take photos of your favorite angles and draw from them while still in the presence of your subject to keep them lively. This exercise can also work well as blind contour drawing (see page 20).

PRACTICE
HERE

SURFACE & TEXTURES

Our tactile experience of our subjects can, and should, affect the way in which we draw them. Distinguishing the fleshiness of skin from the weave of fabric is as much about making textural marks as it is tonal ones.

METAPHOR

Drawing is a visual language that we most often use to describe the things we see, but a drawn mark can also act as a metaphor for a sound, a smell, or the feel of a subject. For instance the sound or intensity of a heartbeat can be represented by its peaks and troughs, but it can also be drawn as abstract marks to show how a heartbeat feels, which can be completely individual depending on the artist. You can make abstract marks on a page in response to things like music, an emotion, or a taste. By making drawings to represent these invisible phenomena, you'll find you start drawing the things you see and can feel physically, differently too.

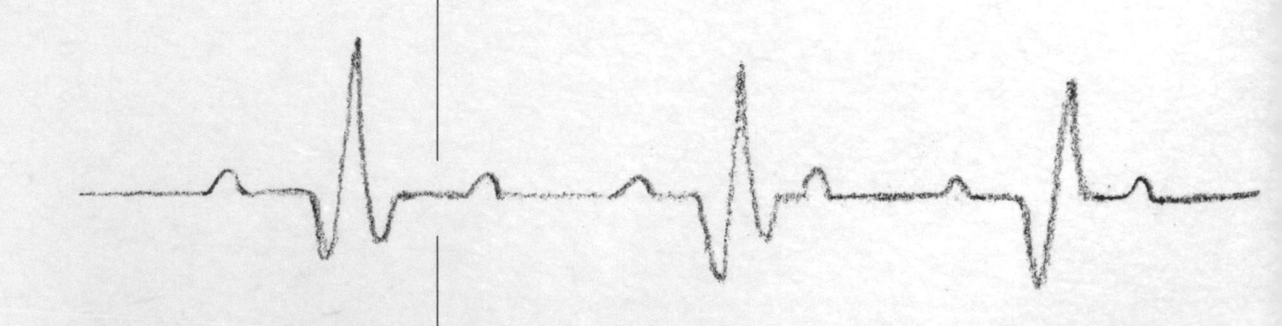

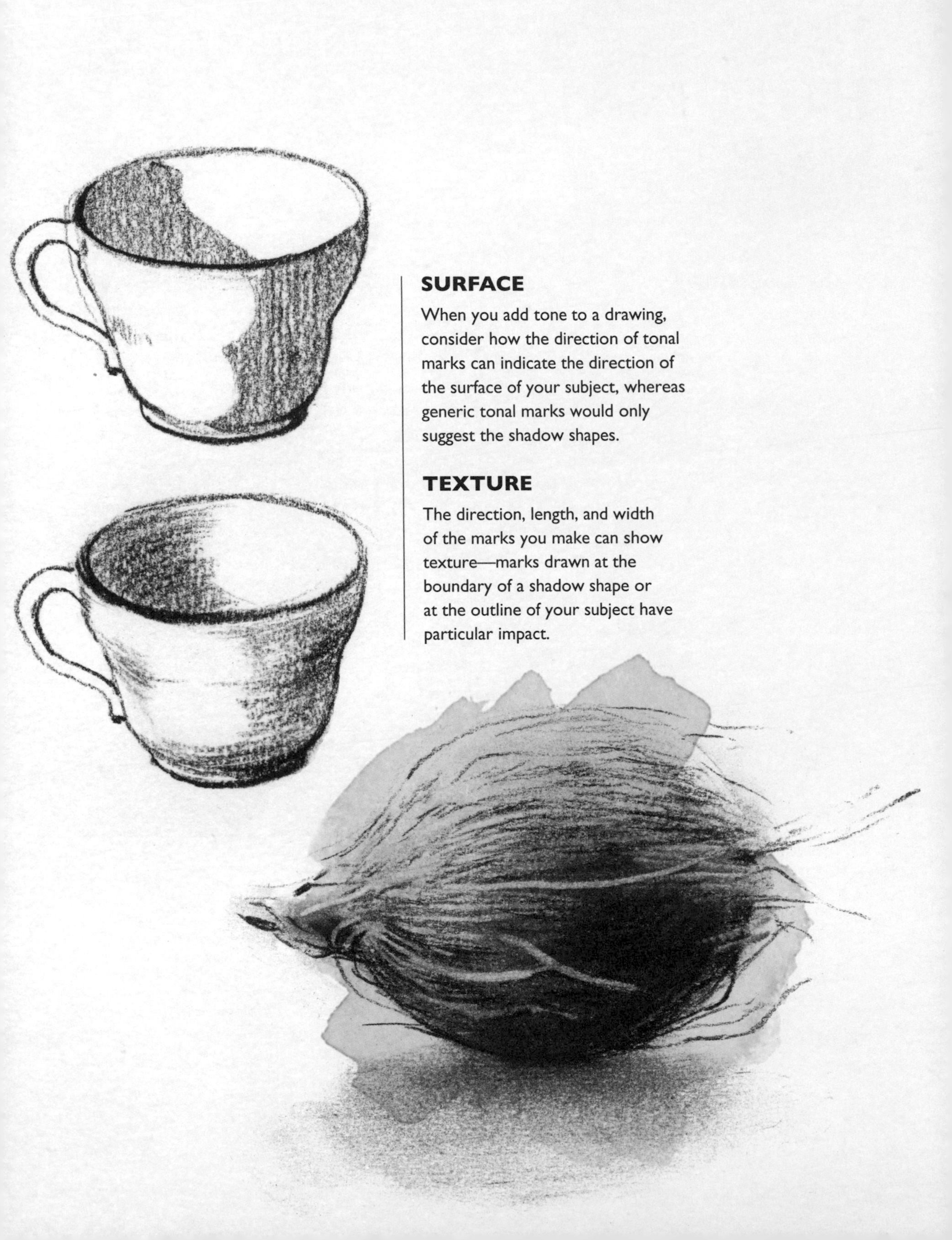

SURFACE

When you add tone to a drawing, consider how the direction of tonal marks can indicate the direction of the surface of your subject, whereas generic tonal marks would only suggest the shadow shapes.

TEXTURE

The direction, length, and width of the marks you make can show texture—marks drawn at the boundary of a shadow shape or at the outline of your subject have particular impact.

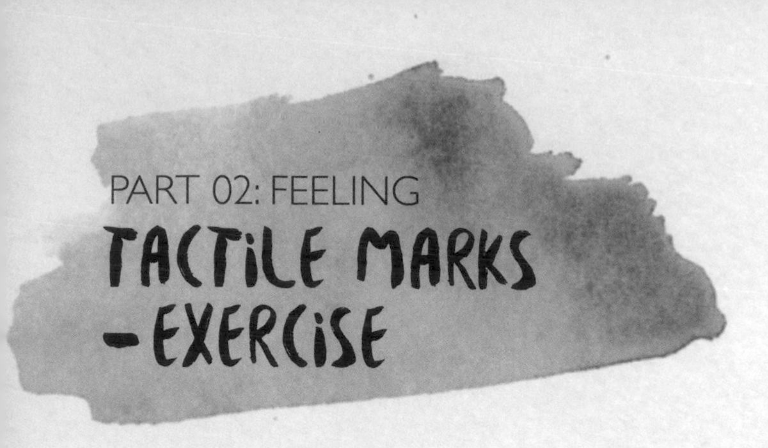

PART 02: FEELING

TACTILE MARKS – EXERCISE

WHAT YOU NEED

- 5 minutes
- Pencil or pen
- Objects in a bag

You don't need to see something to draw it. This exercise is intended to help you experience your subjects on more levels than simply the visual; it is a playful experiment that will strengthen your observed drawings and help you to discover new marks. It works best if you don't know what the object is, so you might want to ask somebody to put an object in the bag for you.

Secure your paper and, with a pencil in your drawing hand, close your eyes and put your other hand in the bag. Feel the shape, weight, and texture of the object and start to make marks, with your eyes still closed. Don't try to draw how you think it looks, just make marks that evoke its surface. When you're finished, look at the drawing—it might look odd, but there will be marks in it that can be transferred into your observed work.

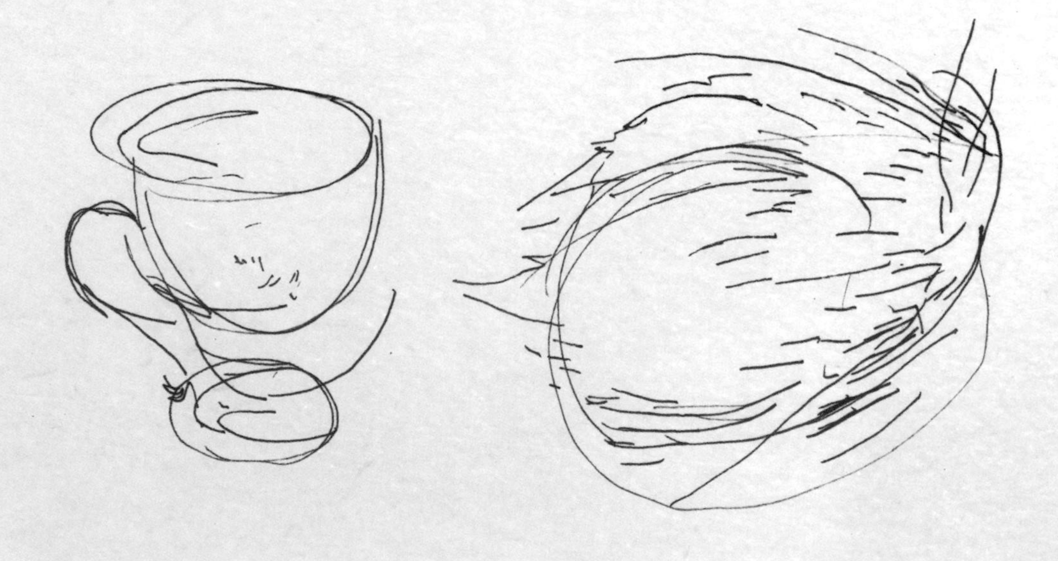

RACTICE
ERE

PART 02: FEELING

BORROWED MARKS

It is often easier to copy a drawing of a face, a figure, or a garden, than it is to draw those subjects from life, because the artist who made the drawing has made all of the decisions for you already—they have picked which lines to accentuate, how darkly to render this shadow or that, and which textural marks to use.

As a result, transcribing somebody else's drawing will allow you to gain a deeper understanding of the marks and processes that went into making it.

TRANSCRIBE TO LEARN

When you copy another artist's drawing you shouldn't just copy the imagery of the picture, but should also aim to replicate every mark; try to emulate the artist's process from beginning to end. You'll learn most when using materials similar to those that the artist used; it will be much more informative to draw from a drawing than it will be to draw from a painting.

BORROW MARKS

Once you have made a few transcriptions and learnt more about how an artist made their marks, you can apply those same marks in your own original drawings. There is nothing wrong with being influenced by other artists' work; if drawing is a language then borrowed marks are just new words to add to your vocabulary. Draw with another artist's marks, assimilate what you like into your own way of working, and disregard what you don't like. If you maintain an honest process of looking and mark-making, you'll be able to borrow from somebody else without jeopardizing your own personal vision—learning to draw like yourself takes a life time and you'll find yourself subject to any number of influences on that journey.

TRANSCRIBING MARKS – EXERCISE

WHAT YOU NEED

- 45 minutes
- Pencil or pen
- A copy of a drawing

Practice transcribing the Vincent van Gogh drawing overleaf onto the opposite page; once you've had a go in this book, find another drawing that you like, print a hard copy and transcribe it into your own sketchbook. You could try the same exercise in a gallery or museum, working from a drawing hung on the wall.

When he was drawing *The Flower Garden*, Van Gogh began by sketching the composition in pencil, building up textural marks in reed pen. Try the same process yourself, starting with a pencil for the initial, light sketch, then drawing over the top in dip pen, or reed pen if you have one. In the absence of a dip or reed pen, you could use a fiber-tip pen or a darker grade of pencil. Then you can apply the marks you have learnt to draw a garden or a pot of flowers from observation, using Van Gogh's marks to inform your own.

(Opposite and page 91 top image detail)
The Flower Garden by Vincent van Gogh, 1888.
Black ink over pencil on paper. Private Collection

PART 02: FEELING

SHAPE, TONE & TEXTURE

When you are drawing a moving, shifting subject like a waterfall, or a sky full of clouds, or an animal, you'll need a sound process to help you deal with the challenge. If you pin down the essential lines of your subject early you can elaborate on tone and texture even as its form changes. Sometimes you'll need to separate the marks you use to suggest tone, form, or texture; sometimes a few marks can suggest all of those qualities at once. Draw shape first, then tone and texture.

This cloud study has been left half-finished. On the left, the clouds begin as simple shapes, drawn as single lines. In the middle of the spread, tone is built up in consistent diagonal marks, and finally, the darkest tonal marks on the right contour around the shape of the clouds, suggesting texture and form.

UP-DO -EXERCISE

WHAT YOU NEED

- 10–45 minutes
- Pencil & eraser
- Drawing overleaf, photograph, or model to copy from

Hair falls in flows of single strands, massing together to create forms that can fall and frizz or be bound and braided. Don't get caught up in drawing individual hairs; instead make sense of the whole mass first, drawing the shapes of the flows in the hair, then finding directional marks that suggest both tone and texture at the same time. Different hair types require a different language of marks.

Copy the drawing overleaf, starting with the outline of the flows and the edges of tonal shapes; then build up marks in the direction of those flows to suggest tone and texture. Add your darkest marks last and erase any final shapes of light. Once you've tried it with this drawing, apply the same approach to a photograph or a model who will pose for you.

1.
2.
3.
4.

RACTICE
ERE

PART 02: FEELING

FABRIC LANDSCAPE – EXERCISE

WHAT YOU NEED

- 45 minutes
- Pencil
- Patterned sheet of fabric

The folded ridges and valleys of a crumpled sheet of fabric make it a satisfying subject for a longer study. The challenges of recording creased cloth can be dealt with one at a time, working from the key folds that define the flow of the fabric to shadow shapes that suggest smaller folds, and ending with a final flourish of distorted pattern.

You'll need to make this drawing in one go—as soon as you move the fabric it will be near impossible to return it to the same position. Drop a sheet of fabric so that it falls into an interesting flow and draw it across the double page spread on pages 104–105. When you add pattern to your drawing, simply draw the shapes that you see, don't try to draw the pattern as you think it would appear flat.

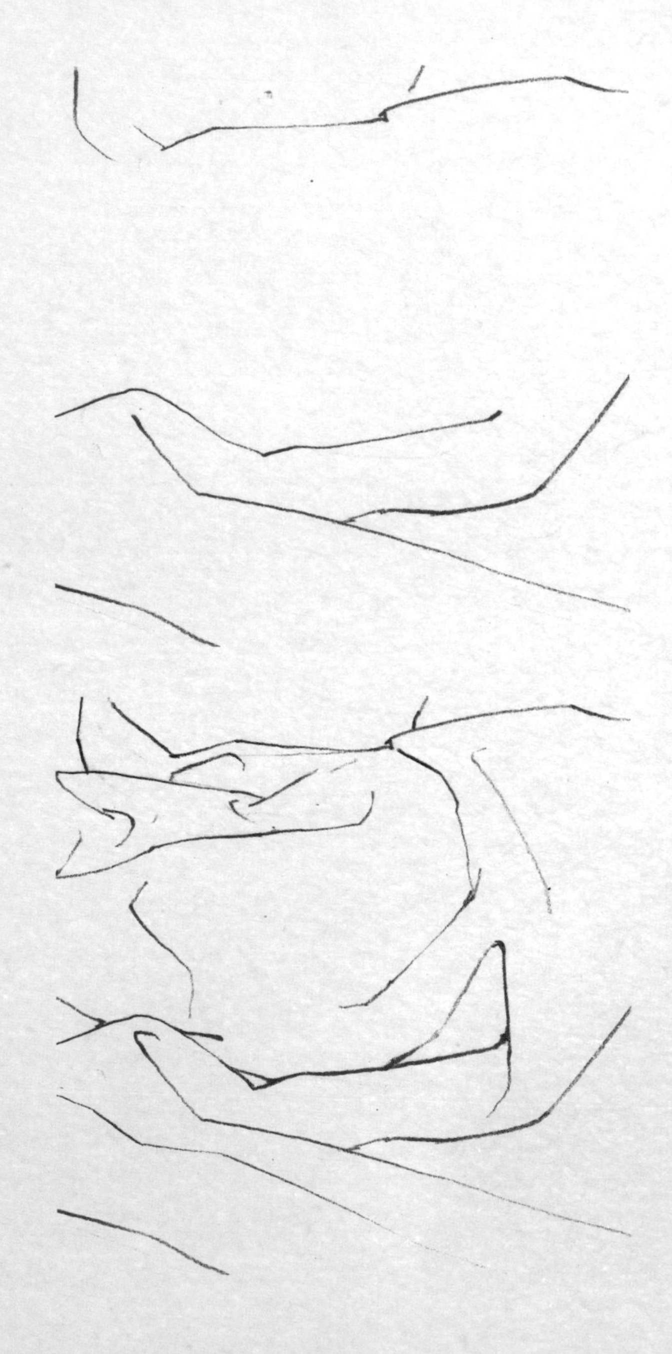

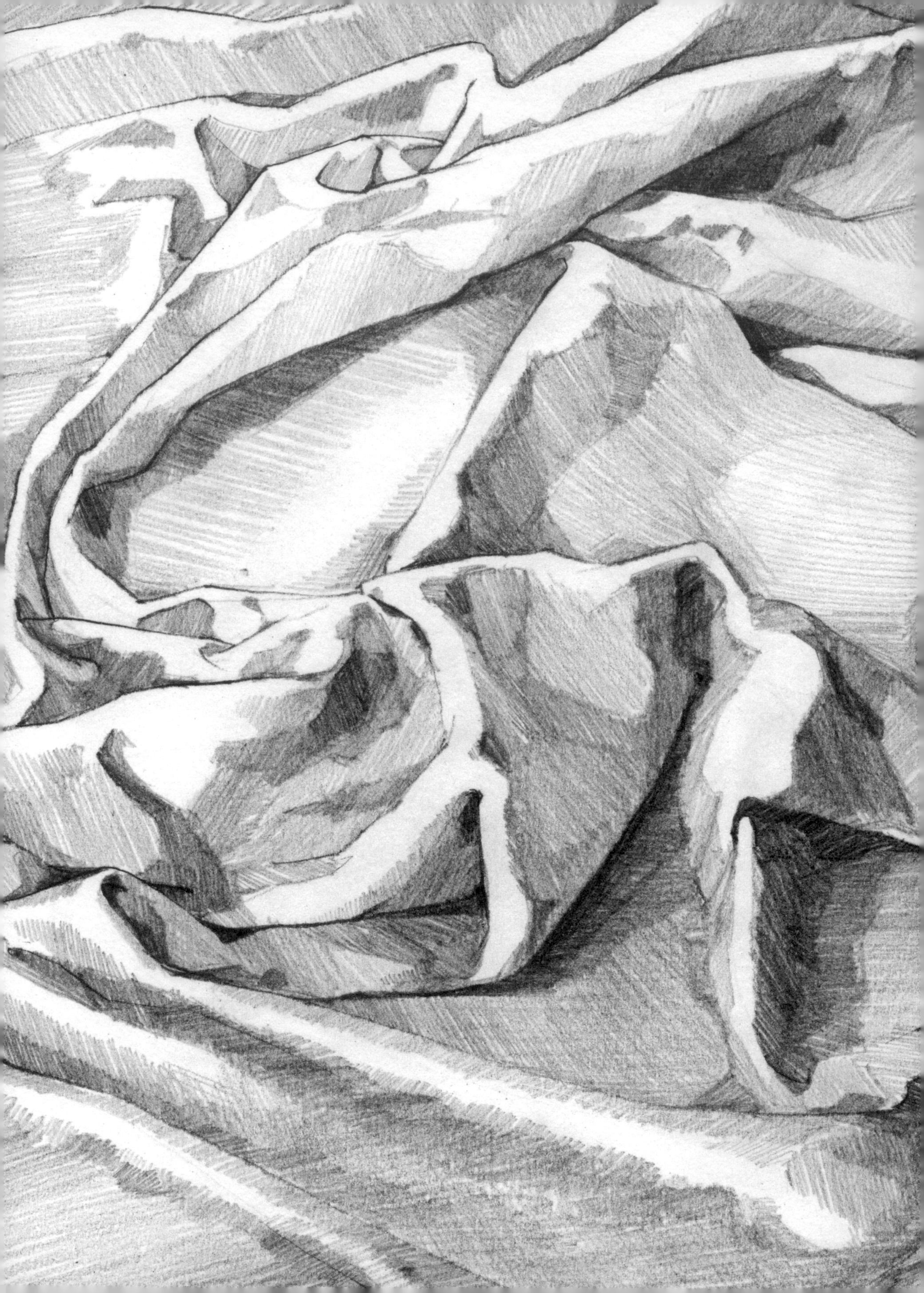

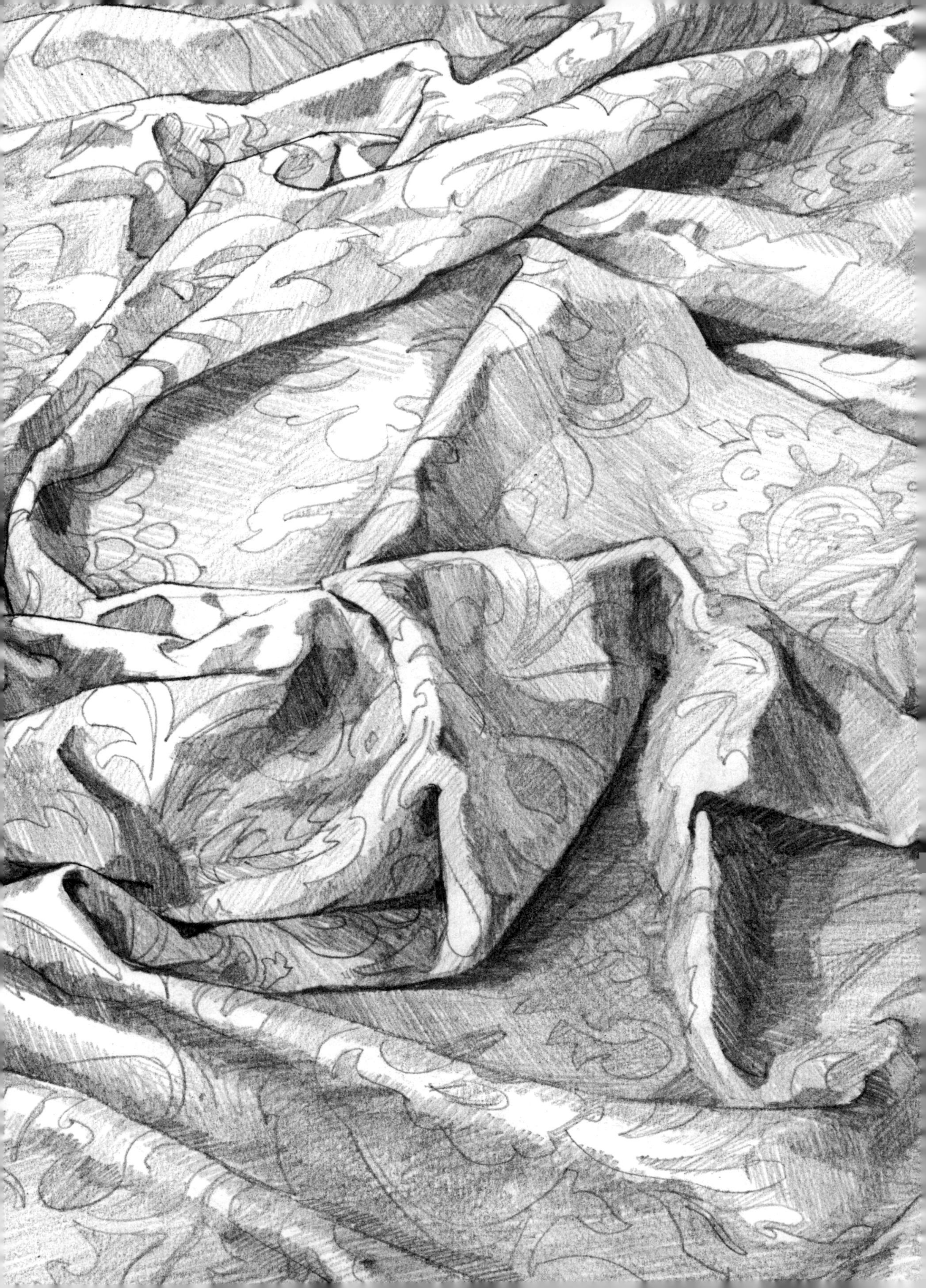

PRACTICE
HERE

PART 02: FEELING

DISTANCE & DETAIL

Drawing distant subjects in less detail than their near equivalents will give your drawings greater depth.

You know that a distant tree is crowned with a mass of tiny leaves so it is easy to get caught up looking for all of that detail, even if all you can really see is a big shape of green. It is only as you get closer that you'll see the texture of the foliage and the negative spaces between branches, and only when you look at a branch up close that you see the shapes of individual leaves. Be economical in your marks and don't make more than you need.

PART 02: FEELING

FOLIAGE – EXERCISE

WHAT YOU NEED

- 1 hour
- Any materials
- Trees or bushes

The methods that you might use to draw bushes and trees can differ depending on how far away you are from them. Find some trees or bushes in full leaf that you can stand back from, and make three drawings.

First, make a drawing of a small branch and a cluster of leaves; look at the shapes of the individual leaves and the spaces between them. Next, stand back so that you can see the whole tree. Draw it, paying attention to the shape of the outline and using repeating textural marks to fill in the tone—just hint at the shape of the leaves. Finally, stand back to see your subject in context with surrounding trees and bushes, and draw it as a simple tonal shape alongside its companions.

PRACTICE
HERE

PART 03

KNOWING

In order to draw well you need to learn to look hard at the world. As you spend more time looking and drawing, your view of the visual world begins to reflect how it really appears: the assumptions that held you back at first can become helpful again.

Seeing and knowing are reciprocal, so that the more you look at a regular subject the better you will understand it, and in turn the better you understand it the clearer you will see it.

SEEING, FEELING, KNOWING

The earlier pages of this book have focused on core skills: skills of perception that help you to see edges, shapes, and tonal value; sympathetic skills to make you aware of the form, gesture, and surface of a subject; mark-making skills to help you develop a visual language. These skills are transferrable across your work and the exercises in Parts 01 and 02 will help you to improve them. This section will help you to put those skills into practice and refine processes for drawing your preferred subjects.

DRAWING TECHNIQUES

A drawing technique is simply a method of working. Just like a recipe in a cook book, there will be basic ingredients—the subject, the materials—and a method to follow. And just like in cooking, there is skill involved in executing the process well, with intuition and experience playing their parts. Some artists shroud their techniques in mystery, like a chef guarding the ingredients of a secret sauce, and the techniques described in books like this one are simplifications intended to be embellished by the reader. Experiment with new techniques you have learned and season them to your taste, adding your own ideas into the mix. Once you have established a technique for approaching a particular subject, either one you have developed yourself or one you have learned, you will find it much less daunting to begin a drawing!

INSIDE OUT VS. OUTSIDE IN

Many techniques use simple shapes to help you structure your observations. There are two common approaches: the first is subtractive and involves drawing big, simple, blocky shapes which you refine like a sculptor chipping away at a block of wood. The second is additive, starting with an internal framework of shapes and lines and building on them, as if you were adding clay to a wire armature. Both approaches work well and some techniques combine both together.

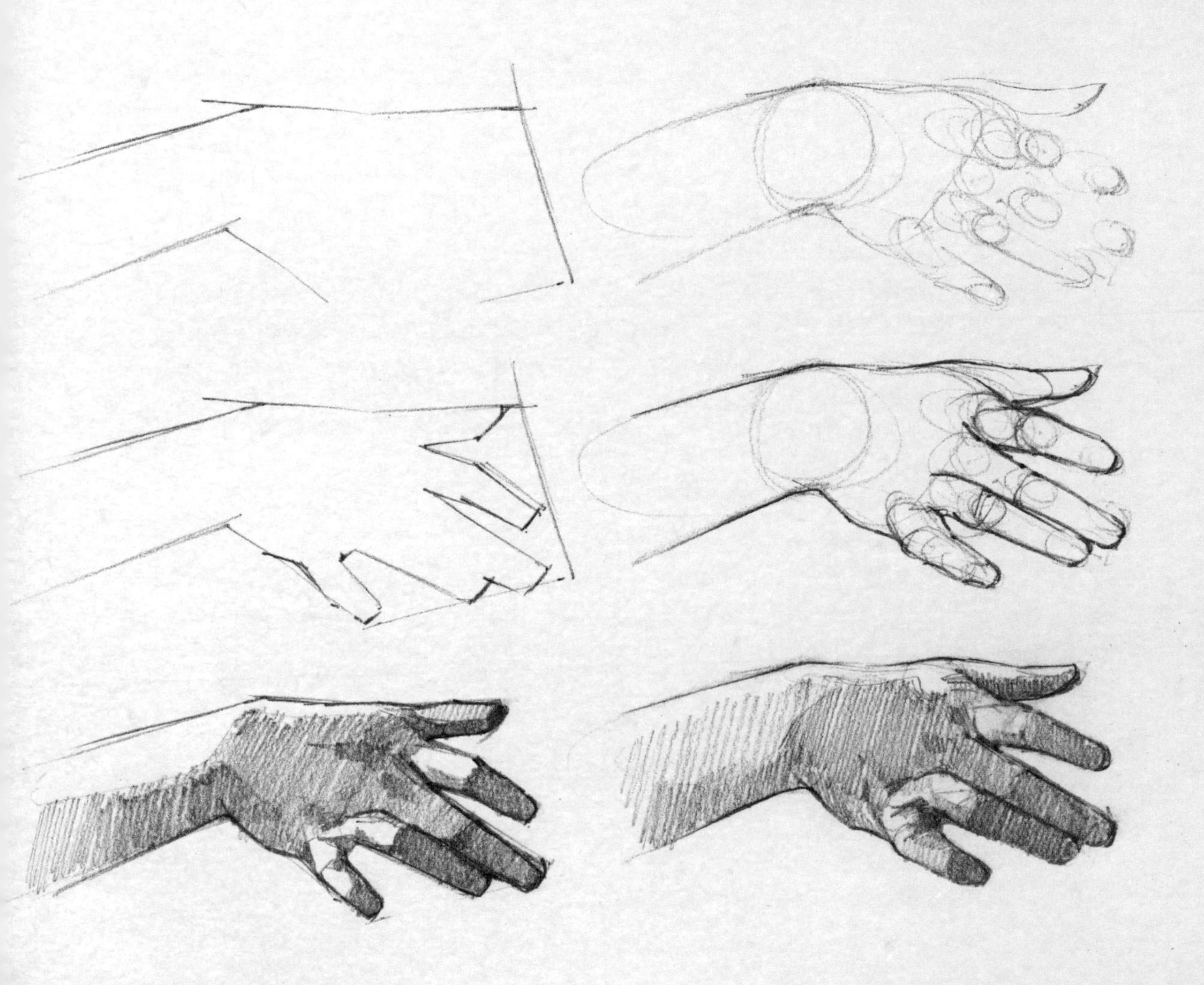

Left: Outside in
Right: Inside out

SHAPES BENEATH THE SKIN

Here is a technique for drawing a hand, that combines an inside out approach with an outside in approach. It starts with a loose sketch, to establish the scale of the drawing, which can be lightly erased before continuing. Chip away at the large shapes to arrive at the finer details of the hand and finish with clear and confident marks over your construction lines.

1.

Establish
Make a quick observational sketch that allows you to look at the whole hand and establish the scale of the drawing.

2.

Big shapes
Use straight marks to draw the simplified mass of the whole hand, as if you were carving it from wood.

3.

Landmarks
Draw in the key joints of the wrist and knuckles as loose, lightly-sketched circles to establish the landmarks of the hand.

4.

Negative spaces
Refine the drawing further and draw in the negative spaces between fingers.

5.

Line
Partially erase your construction lines and, using them for guidance, draw the edges that you see around the hand with a varied and lively line.

6.

Tone
Loosely sketch in the shadows that give the hand form, contouring the surface with your marks.

PART 03: KNOWING

HANDS – EXERCISE

WHAT YOU NEED

- 15 minutes
- HB & 2B pencils
- Your hand

Construction lines help you to map out your drawing; by making these initial lines in a hard, pale grade of pencil you'll avoid making heavy marks too early, allowing your final lines to have greater impact.

Sit down at a table; make sure that your book won't move around (you can secure paper to the table with masking tape if you are drawing on a loose sheet) and, with your HB pencil in your drawing hand, hold your non-drawing hand in a pose, making sure it is well lit. Work through the process suggested on the previous spread, constantly flicking your eyes between hand and page and, when you are satisfied with the proportions of your construction, switch to a 2B pencil to draw the observed edges and tone onto the underlying structure. Make studies of different hand poses over the next few pages; you can also try this exercise in the mirror or ask somebody else to model for you to give you a variety of angles.

PRACTICE
HERE

PRACTICE
HERE

PART 03: KNOWING

SIDEWAYS GLANCE – EXERCISE

WHAT YOU NEED

- 5–20 minutes
- Pencil & eraser
- A head in profile

The head in profile presents a clear edge to be drawn and doesn't demand the symmetry of a face-on portrait. As your subject will be looking away from you, this can also make for a more relaxed and informal process than a posed, front-on portrait. You can find various opportunities to sketch your models as they sit on the bus, in cafés, or in front of the television.

This exercise involves working from the inside out, building up the face from simple shapes that give a rough idea of the anatomy of the head. Rather than beginning with a generic oval, sketch in the skull and neck as your establishing shapes. Jot in some quick proportional marks that can be easily erased, as scaffolding on which to hang the features. Lightly erase the entire construction drawing, so that you can still see faintly the marks on the page. Then develop the face from the eye socket, using the eyebrow as a starting point. Navigate the face in small jumps, from feature to feature, rather than launching into the line of the profile right away. On the spread overleaf you'll find step-by-step guidance to help you.

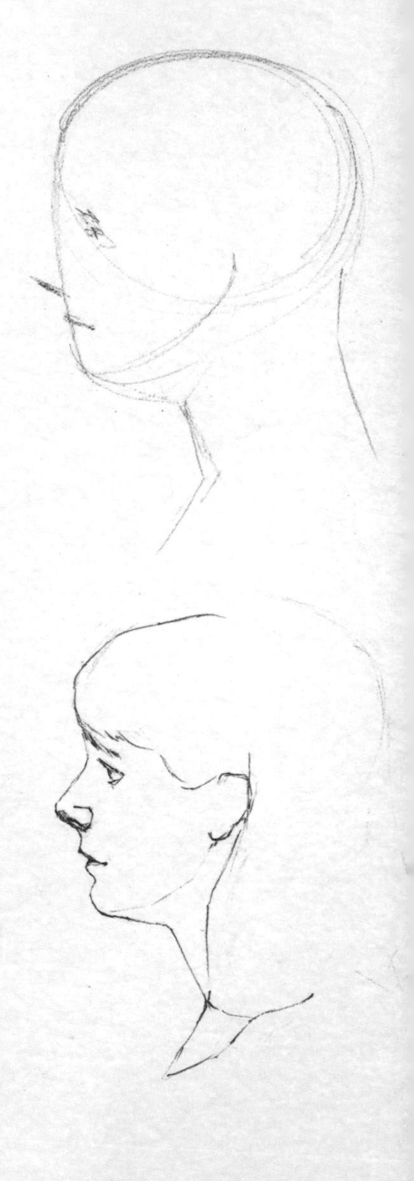

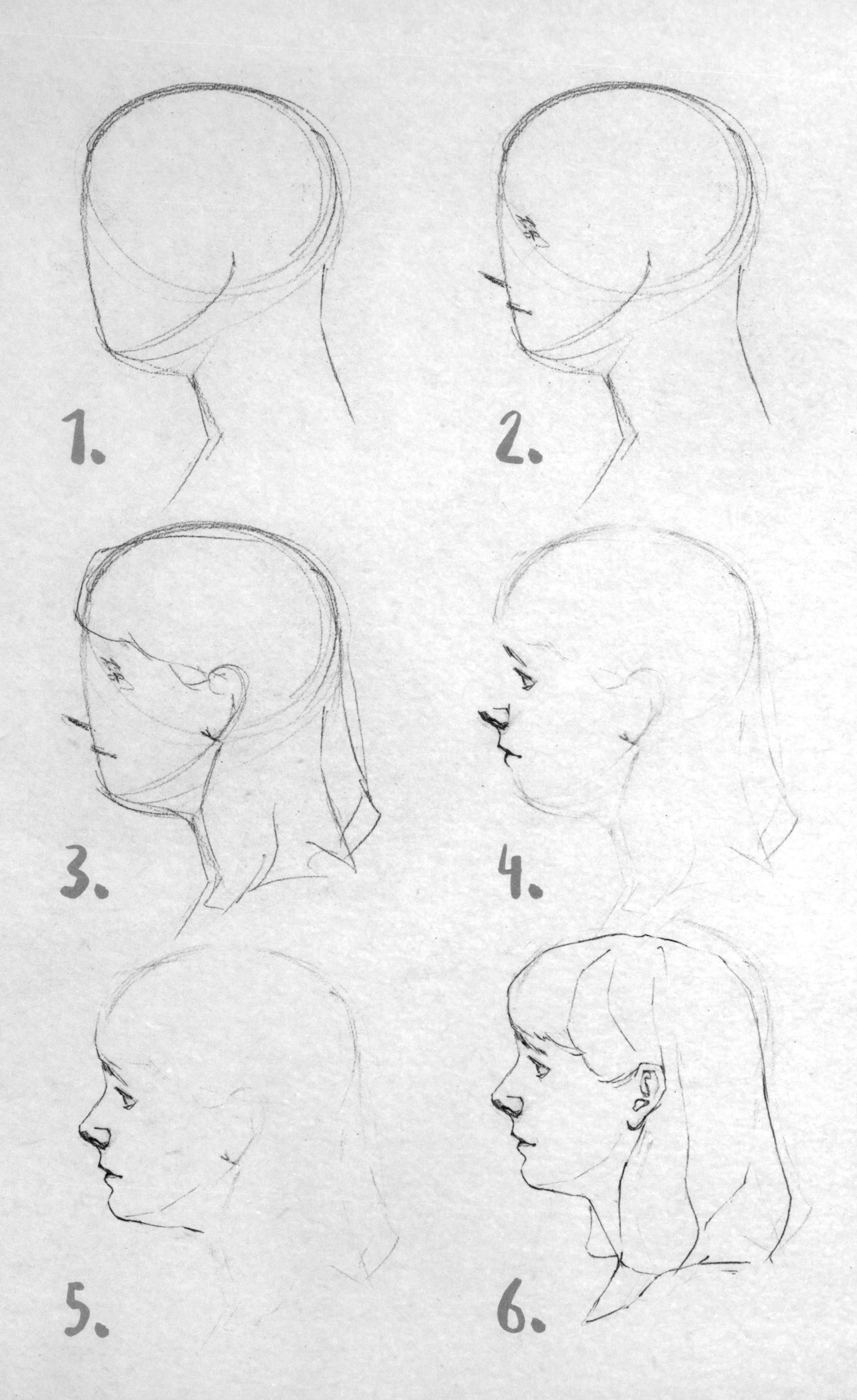
1.
2.
3.
4.
5.
6.

PART 03: KNOWING

PERSPECTIVE

The principles of perspective will help you to create the illusion of three-dimensional space on a two-dimensional surface. Although you don't need to know any of these principles to draw what you see, a little knowledge can help you to anticipate the visual effects that play out in front of you, as well as giving you a framework on which you can build imagined spaces. You'll find that different effects of perspective will present themselves more prominently with particular subject matter, so you can prepare yourself as best as possible when faced with a challenging drawing.

The next few pages touch on some basics of perspective—use these as a foundation to learn more.

FORESHORTENING

The term "foreshortening" is usually used to describe the effects of perspective on a single subject. When a subject appears foreshortened, the length along your line of sight appears relatively shorter than the same length across your line of sight. An example of this distortion of scale can be seen below, where a recumbent figure is drawn from a low viewpoint —the nearby foot appears larger than you might expect and the distant head much smaller. When you are drawing a particularly foreshortened subject, use the measuring techniques suggested on pages 126–127 to help you plot your drawing accurately.

DISTANCE & SCALE

The farther away your subject, the smaller it will appear; you'll notice this when you are drawing lots of similar-sized subjects in a wide space. Jotting in the top and bottom limits of your subjects will really help you to proportion them.

COLOR & TONE

The nearer your subjects are, the more vivid their colors appear, the brighter the light tones, and the darker the dark tones. Atmospheric distortions cause distant objects to appear less tonally distinct, paler and bluer.

This will be most evident when you are looking across vast spaces in landscape drawing or when drawing on a misty day. The effects of atmospheric perspective can be emphasized to create drama in your work.

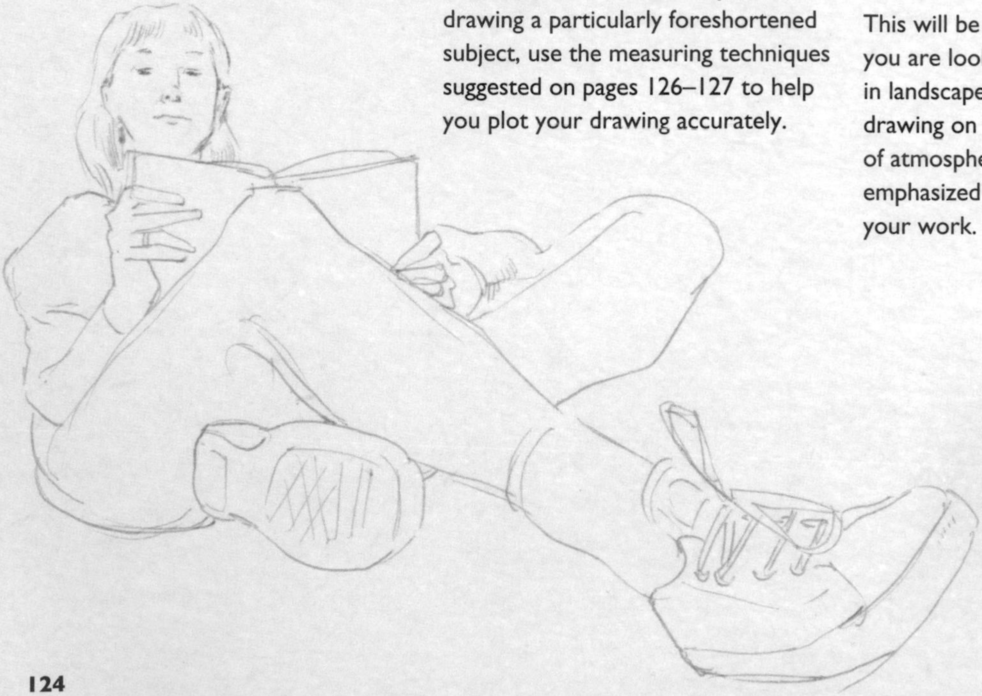

PART 03: KNOWING

MEASURING TOOLS – MATERIALS

Estimating proportions by eye will train you to make more accurate judgments. However, a few simple tools can be used to aid your observational measuring. A pencil, straight edge, or plumb line will be your most useful measuring tools.

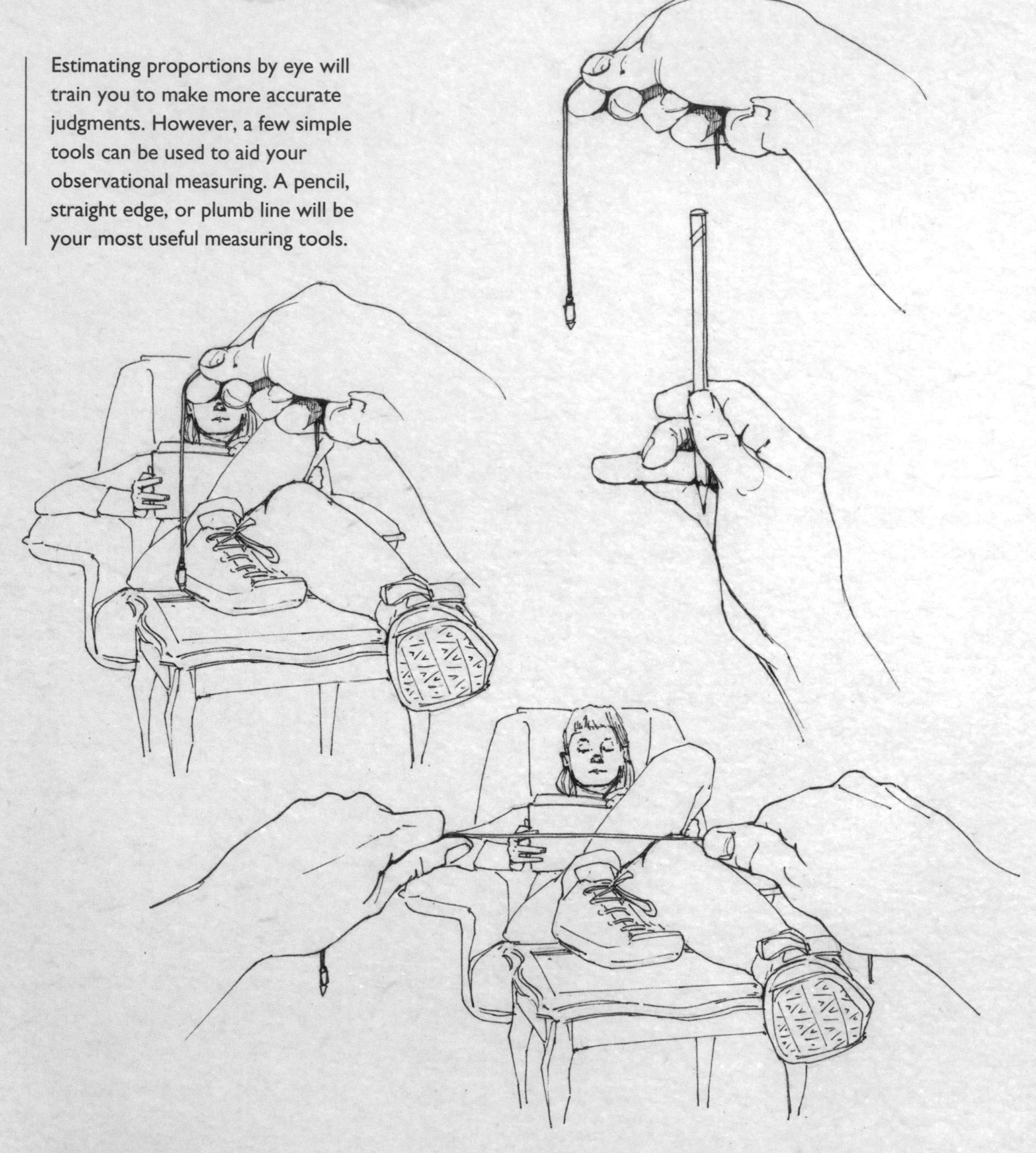

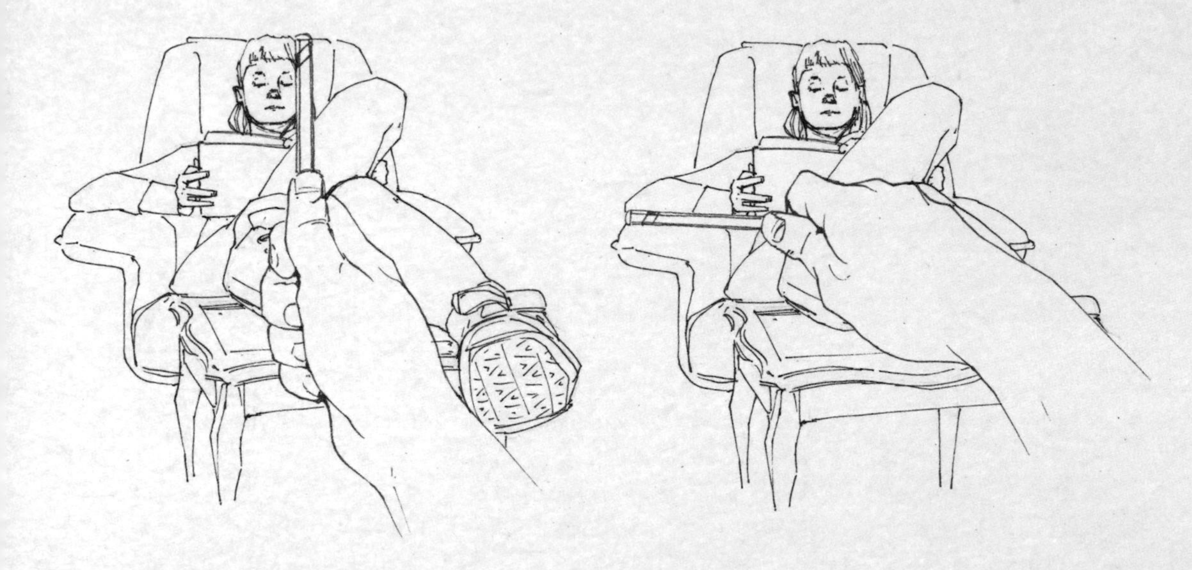

MEASURING DISTANCES

Line up the top of your pencil with something you want to measure. Run your thumb down to take a measurement. You can then compare this measurement to other parts of your subject and check the proportional ratio against your drawing—this is called comparative measuring. Sight size measuring is where you draw your subject the exact size that you see it.

CHECKING ANGLES

Close one eye to flatten what you see and, holding your pencil out at arm's length, line up the edge of the pencil with an edge on your subject to check you have the same corresponding angle in your drawing.

PART 03: KNOWING

THE BODY AS LANDSCAPE – EXERCISE

WHAT YOU NEED

- 15–30 minutes
- Pencil, eraser & viewfinder
- A reclining figure

A view across a body, seen from an extreme angle, can seem more like a landscape than a figure. Drawing the figure from unusual angles will train your eyes to look for unexpected shapes and provides an opportunity to practice observational measuring. This exercise works well for drawing sunbathing friends on a beach, long reclining poses in a life-drawing class, or your family lying on the sofa.

Find a challenging angle to draw from, looking across the body. Mark in lightly the top, bottom, left, and right extremes of the pose and, as described on the previous page, use your pencil to check the height against the width of your subject—correct the drawing if necessary. Draw the biggest shapes of the figure first, drawing negative spaces and surrounding furniture to help you check proportions.

PRACTICE
HERE

ONE-POINT PERSPECTIVE

Linear perspective relies on the principle that two parallel lines, receding away from the viewer, appear to converge on a distant horizon line. The point at which they disappear is called the vanishing point.

Although nature exhibits few straight lines that disappear neatly in this way, the man-made environment is full of them. As most of our buildings and roads are built on grids, with their vertical edges aligned with gravity and their horizontal planes parallel to the earth, we see these lines everywhere.

A drawing made using one-point perspective has just a single vanishing point and is used when you are flat on to one plane of your subject. Imagine you are looking into the room through a huge pane of glass that makes up one wall—this is the flat plane from which lines from the edge of the room will extend away to the vanishing point, interrupted by the plane of the wall opposite. As long as all of the furniture in the room is aligned with one edge facing your glass wall, then the same, single vanishing point on the horizon that you used to draw the room can be used to draw the furniture in perspective.

DRAW A ROOM AND FURNITURE OVER THE GUIDE STRUCTURE HERE

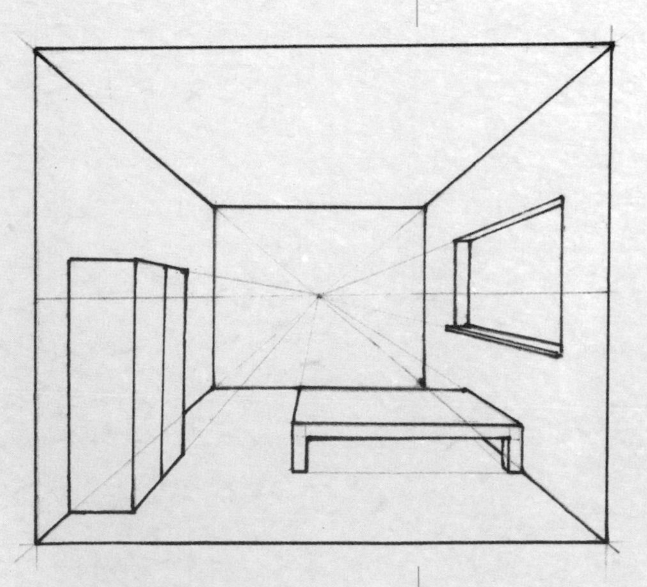

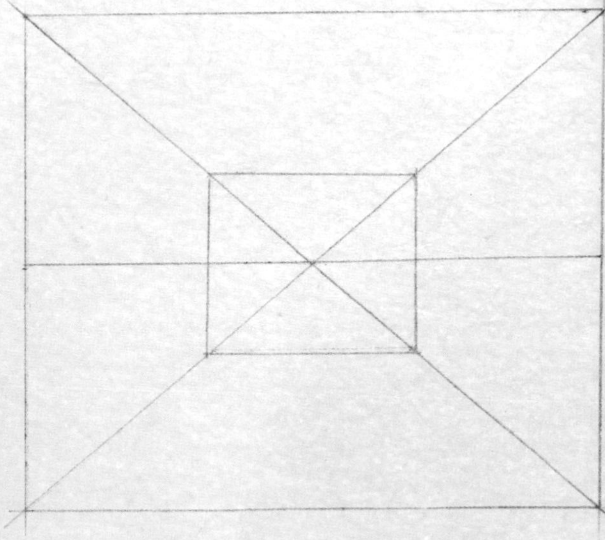

Changing the position of the horizon line or vanishing point in relation to the plane of your vision will give you a different view of your subject.

EXPLORE DRAWING SIMPLE BLOCKS IN AN IMAGINARY SPACE THAT CONFORM TO THE PRINCIPLES OF PERSPECTIVE

PART 03: KNOWING

TWO-POINT PERSPECTIVE

When you are standing edge on at a corner of a regular, box-like shape, you will see two sets of parallel lines that recede to different vanishing points—one set in one direction, one in the other. Those vanishing points might end up extending off your page.

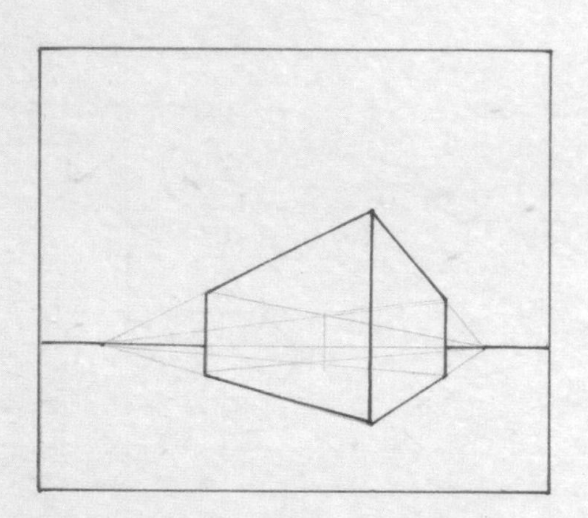

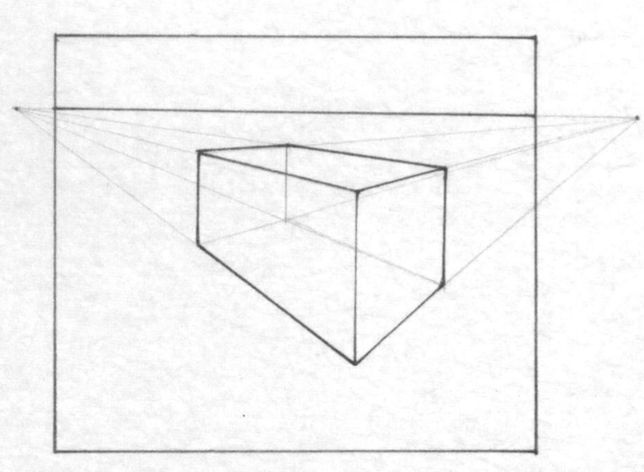

DRAW A HORIZON LINE AND ADD TWO POINTS TO IT. THEN JOIN THE POINTS TO DRAW A BUILDING, AS ABOVE

The basics of linear perspective can help you to construct imaginary three-dimensional spaces on your page, but they'll also be useful in helping you resolve problems in your observational drawings. When you are sketching in a built environment you can use your pencil to estimate the angles of receding parallel lines and roughly judge a vanishing point, then use these to structure other parts of your drawing. There is much more to learn about perspective than these basic rules—read up to understand some of its finer points.

PART 03: KNOWING

AN URBAN SKETCH – EXERCISE

WHAT YOU NEED

- Plenty of time
- Pencil, eraser & pen
- Buildings

A cluster of buildings offers an ideal subject for applying the principles of perspective. The repeating regular shapes of the man-made environment can take some time to draw, so prepare to spend a little while drawing.

First, make sure that you are sitting comfortably and spend a moment looking for an interesting composition (see page 144). Then start drawing by blocking out on the page the largest shapes of the view in front of you; don't worry about perspective yet. Once you have jotted down a rough composition, find a set of receding parallel lines and trace them back to their vanishing point, which could easily be off the page, on the horizon line, which will most likely be hidden from view! Use these lines as a starting point to work out how other lines fit in relation to them, and use this linear structure as a scaffold on which to build your drawing. Make a sketch on the spread overleaf, beginning in pencil and finishing in pen.

PRACTICE
HERE

PART 04

SELECTING

Drawing is a selective process. The conscious or intuitive selection of materials, subjects, and marks that you make as you draw creates outcomes that are unique to you and your vision of the world.

When you are developing basic skills you'll be consumed with the "how" of drawing but, as you become more confident, you'll be able to concentrate on the "why." Knowing why you are making a drawing can both take pressure off your practice and help you to improve. Before you start a drawing ask yourself what the drawing is about and what it is for; a clear intention will help you to decide on what approach to take.

DRAWING AS RECORD

The long moment of looking that drawing affords you can help fix the things you see in your memory. Simple thumbnail sketches serve as mnemonics to help you remember a scene that could become a more considered drawing later. Sketches done while travelling can transport you back to the moment in which you made them. A drawing made as a record is often for you alone and the roughest sketches can be valuable mementos.

DRAWING AS PROCESS

Sometimes drawing can simply be a physical process that helps you look more intently or allows you to practice making marks. You might use observational drawing or abstract mark-making as a form of meditation. When you are led by process, you don't need to judge yourself on the outcome of the work.

DRAWING AS LANGUAGE

Drawing crosses language barriers and can be the best way to describe a visual or spatial idea. Signage is pure visual communication, comic strips tell stories through sequential images, and an architect's drawing contains directions for engineers and builders. A drawing made to communicate something is often judged on the clarity of its message more than on the poetry of its execution.

DRAWING AS INVENTION

A drawing can be a conduit for the imagination; character designs, concepts for new furniture, or compositions for paintings can make their first contact with the world through your sketchbook. Some ideas seem to form themselves almost instantly on the page in front of you, while others are developed over many iterations. Inventive drawings are often fragmented and playful—what they lack in representational accuracy, they make up for in imaginative potential.

DRAWING AS ART-MAKING

The skills of looking and mark-making that define the process of drawing can also be used in painting, printmaking, sculpture, filmmaking, or photography, and the sensibilities of drawing could be explored in all of these media. A drawing can be an artwork in itself, whether created for that purpose or labeled as artwork later, and it is as "art" that a drawing is most readily critiqued. Whether a drawing is a good artwork or not will depend entirely on the context in which it is presented. That isn't to say you can't assess the quality of a drawing, it is simply that the success of a drawing is relative to its intention and its presentation.

PART 04: SELECTING

THE PICTURE PLANE

The picture plane is the space within which your image is drawn. The four edges of your page initially define your picture plane, but you can choose to work within different dimensions by drawing a box on your page to contain your sketch.

The dimensions and orientation of your picture plane will radically alter how you compose your drawing—if your subject suits a long, slim, landscape format, then draw a long, slim box across the page to sketch in. If your subject suits a square picture plane, then draw a square box on the page, and so on.

COMPOSITION

Composition is the arrangement of contrasting masses within a picture plane. You compose drawings unconsciously without having to be aware of the formal principles of composition—you might look at a subject that you intend to draw and adjust your viewpoint subtly until the image in front of you clicks into place and just feels right. Once you have drawn it, you might find that the image conforms to many of the principles of good composition. Well-considered composition will help to lead the viewer's eyes around a drawing, allowing you to create narrative in an image and direct attention.

ARMATURES

Simple lines sketched onto the picture plane can help you to plan a composition, supporting the drawing like a wire armature supports a clay sculpture. To test compositions, reduce your subject to a few essential lines first to see the overall layout of how the drawing would look, and to understand another artist's compositions better—redraw their work in a handful of simple marks.

CROPPING

If you want to alter the picture plane as you draw, you can always partially erase it and either extend it or reduce it. Experiment with different crops of the same subject to achieve very different drawings.

PART 04: SELECTING

THUMBNAILS – EXERCISE

WHAT YOU NEED

- 10 minutes each day
- Viewfinder & pencil
- Any subject

Interesting compositions can be found everywhere when you take the time to look. Observe the world through eyes that are hungry for interesting shapes and practice making daily compositional sketches.

A cardboard viewfinder (see page 30) will help you look for compositions in the same way that a camera viewfinder helps a photographer. Hold your viewfinder in front of you and search for an interesting composition to sketch. You are not just looking for an engaging subject; you are looking for an interesting collection of shapes within the aperture of the viewfinder. Quickly sketch the shapes and tones of what you see, without overworking the detail of the subject. Save the interesting compositions in your book and when you feel like making a longer drawing, return to the subject and make a more developed sketch. On the next spread, draw a small composition every day for ten days, and try more thumbnails on pages 148–149.

PRACTICE HERE

PRACTICE
HERE

PART 04: SELECTING

GOOD HABITS

There are many established conventions of composition that you can employ to better compose your drawings. These conventions can be presented as rules, but it is better to think of them as providing an insight into good and bad habits when designing compositions. You can research these conventions further if you find them helpful and, by looking critically at the work of other artists, you can borrow their ideas to apply to your own work. Here are some considerations to start you off.

BALANCE TONAL SHAPES

To construct an effective composition you will need to think beyond the subjects of the drawing and consider how simple shapes of light and dark interact on the page. For example, in the drawing above you can see the trees as blocks of dark midtone—the large tree on the right creates a heavy shape that is balanced by the cluster on the left, with the line of the brow of the hill connecting them across the center of the page.

LEAD THE EYE

Effective composition will lead the eye on a journey through the drawing. As you plan your composition, think about where somebody might be inclined to look first and where their eyes might travel. This drawing was intended to lead the viewer to three hidden figures in the middle of the page. It is natural for the eye to enter at the wide base of the path and either go straight upward, guided by the hanging plants and lamppost, or to zigzag up the path, stopped by the heavy black shape at the end, then back along the top of the wall, coming to rest on the figures.

PART 04: SELECTING

ABSTRACTION – EXERCISE

WHAT YOU NEED

- 15 minutes
- Preferred medium
- Compositional sketches

To abstract is to "draw out from." Abstraction strips drawing back to its fundamental components: when a drawing can no longer be relied on as an accurate representation of the imagery it evokes, its success will hinge on engaging marks and effective composition.

For this exercise you'll need to photocopy the compositional sketches you made on pages 146–147.

Take one of the sketches, turn it upside down and place it next to this book. Pick a small section of the upside-down sketch and redraw it on page 154, simplifying it into simple tonal shapes. Put away the original composition. Now redraw the new composition on page 155, using a variety of marks. Think about how masses of tone or pattern relate to one another and how different marks create abstract textures. Alter the drawing until it works as well as possible as an arrangement of interesting shapes and marks. Develop your own process for abstracting your drawings or looking at them in unconventional ways.

PRACTICE
HERE

WHAT'S NEXT?

Once you have filled this book, make sure you are well prepared to keep drawing. If you have worked through each exercise, with extra practice outside of the book, then you will have laid down a good foundation on which to build your drawing skills. You now need to make it easy for yourself to continue, removing the barriers that might stop you from drawing.

TIME

Set some time aside in the week to draw. Join a drawing group, arrange to meet a friend to draw together, carry your sketchbook with you everywhere so that you can make use of brief sketching opportunities.

CONFIDENCE

Make the decision to continue drawing and accept that this will mean lots of practice before you become fluent and confident in your approach. Enjoy the process of learning and memorize your favorite exercises from this book so that you can practice them regularly.

MATERIALS & SUBJECT

Put a small drawing set together: a sketchbook and a pencil case of your favorite materials that you can carry with you everywhere. If you don't have these with you, improvise with found materials and stick the scraps in your sketchbook later. Use pages 6–9 to find exercises suitable for your location or the subjects you are interested in.

FULL MATERIALS LIST

YOU WILL NEED

- Graphite pencils
- Eraser
- Sharpener
- Willow charcoal
- Charcoal pencil
- Fixative
- Ballpoint pen
- Fiber-tip pen
- Dip pen/reed pen
- Indian ink
- Tissue
- Viewfinder
- Steel rule
- Craft knife
- Cutting mat
- Cardboard

REFERENCES & ACKNOWLEDGMENTS

Thank you to everybody who has contributed to this book, to all of the Brighton drawing community without whom it would not have been possible, and John T. Freeman, an artist of substance and integrity. Thank you also to the models who posed for drawings in this book: Amy Squirrel, Naomi Wood, Laura Ryan, Mary Martin, Bella Franks, Laura Kate O'Rourke, Felix Clement, Francesca Cluney, Shelley Morrow, and to Ian and Jenny Bailey for hosting a wonderful sketching trip to Portugal. Thank you to Jennie Webber at Wild Life Drawing for providing the lovely owls, to the anonymous cat that I drew prowling around for Chasing Tails, and to Martin Christie whose photograph inspired a drawing. I'd also like to give special thanks to Nic de Jesus whose advice led to the sea drawing exercises and to Hester Berry who gave me a love of clouds. Finally, thank you to Zara, Rachel and Francesca, and all of the staff at Ilex who, along with the designers, have shaped the book from inception to completion.

RECOMMENDED READING

Keys to Drawing by Bert Dodgson (for all-round drawing advice)

Drawing Projects by Jack Southern and Mick Maslen (for theory and practice)

Draw by Jake Spicer (to help you draw as part of your daily life)

Portrait Drawing by John T. Freeman (for portrait drawing instruction)

The Drawing Book by Sarah Simblet (for an informed overview of drawing)

The Art of Urban Sketching by Gabriel Campanario (for inspiration for sketching on location)

Van Gogh Drawings, Dover Art Library (for more drawings to copy)

WEB & SOCIAL MEDIA

www.draw-brighton.co.uk
(drawing classes in Brighton, UK)

www.urbansketchers.org
(international sketching network)

www.thebigdraw.org
(international drawing charity)

www.jakespicerart.co.uk
@BrightonDrawing
#jakespicer